THE MARNE
1914

French infantry.

THE MARNE
1914
A Battlefield Guide

Andrew Uffindell

Pen & Sword
MILITARY

First published in Great Britain in 2013 by
P E N   &   S W O R D   M I L I T A R Y
an imprint of
Pen & Sword Books Ltd
47 Church Street
Barnsley
South Yorkshire
S70 2AS

ISBN 978-1-84884-801-6

A CIP catalogue record for this book
is available from the British Library

Typeset in 10/12.5pt Palatino by
Concept, Huddersfield

Printed and bound in India by
Replika Press Pvt. Ltd.

*Pen & Sword Books Ltd incorporates the Imprints of Pen & Sword
Aviation, Pen & Sword Family History, Pen & Sword Maritime,
Pen & Sword Military, Pen & Sword Discovery, Wharncliffe Local
History, Wharncliffe True Crime, Wharncliffe Transport, Pen & Sword
Select, Pen & Sword Military Classics, Leo Cooper, The Praetorian Press,
Remember When, Seaforth Publishing and Frontline Publishing.*

For a complete list of Pen & Sword titles please contact
PEN & SWORD BOOKS LIMITED
47 Church Street, Barnsley, South Yorkshire, S70 2AS, England
E-mail: enquiries@pen-and-sword.co.uk
Website: www.pen-and-sword.co.uk

CONTENTS

ACKNOWLEDGEMENTS

For their encouragement during the writing of this book, I am much indebted to my family and friends. As always, Rupert Harding and the team at Pen and Sword Books have been unfailingly helpful and supportive, and I am grateful to Sarah Cook for all her work in editing the book. I am grateful also to the staff at Hertfordshire County Library Services, the British Library, the National Archives at Kew, the *Deutsche Nationalbibliothek* at Leipzig, the *Bibliothèque nationale de France* at Paris, and the *Service historique de la défense* at Vincennes.

I am much obliged to Pascale Belouis of the *Syndicat d'Initiative de Gagny* for information about the taxis plaque, and to Daniel Patillet, who kindly permitted me to quote from the remarkable eyewitness account of his grandfather, *Caporal* Henri Bury of the *276e régiment*. (Bury's account can be found online at: www.padage.free.fr.) I also wish to thank Philippe Braquet for welcoming me to his museum at Villeroy, the *Sœurs Oblates de St François de Sales* for their kindness in letting me visit the *Maison du père Brisson* at Plancy, Jacques Ferrenbach for showing me inside Neufmontiers church, the *maire* of Normée for opening its church for me, and the many inhabitants throughout the battlefield area for their more general helpfulness.

French infantry attack.

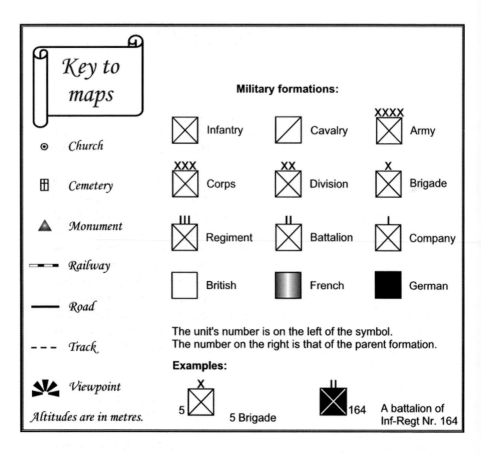

Key to maps

⊙ *Church*

⊞ *Cemetery*

▲ *Monument*

🚂 *Railway*

— *Road*

- - - *Track*

🔅 *Viewpoint*

Altitudes are in metres.

Military formations:

⊠ Infantry

◪ Cavalry

XXXX ⊠ Army

XXX ⊠ Corps

XX ⊠ Division

X ⊠ Brigade

III ⊠ Regiment

II ⊠ Battalion

I ⊠ Company

☐ British

▨ French

■ German

The unit's number is on the left of the symbol.
The number on the right is that of the parent formation.

Examples:

5 ⊠ X   5 Brigade

■II 164   A battalion of Inf-Regt Nr. 164

INTRODUCTION

The Marne is one of the most pivotal battles in history. Fought outside Paris in September 1914, it turned the tide of the German invasion of France, and robbed *Kaiser* Wilhelm II of his best chance of winning the First World War.

The battle took its name from the river that flows westwards in a great arc, 525 km long, to join the Seine immediately south-east of Paris. Various other possibilities were suggested when the French headquarters discussed what to call it. The 'Paris–Verdun battle' sounded too much like a motorcar race, while the 'Battle of the Catalaunian Fields' was deemed too scholarly, being a reference to Attila the Hun's defeat in the same region almost 1,500 years earlier. In contrast, the Marne was more appropriate: the river not only linked the various sectors of the battlefield, but also set the seal on the outcome, for it was when the British and French breached the line of the river on 9 September – the climax of the battle – that they forced the Germans to retreat.

Even during the war, soldiers were struck by the beauty of the Marne valley. 'We saw a picture of the deepest peace,' wrote *Vizefeldwebel* Adolf Schwenzer of the *Garde-Jäger-Bataillon*, 'picturesque villages, ranges of hills covered in vineyards, and, in between, the silver ribbon of the Marne, lit by a blue, sunny sky.' He was echoed by one of his enemies, a British subaltern. 'It was a perfect morning, and there was not a sign of any living person,' the subaltern recalled. 'Everything seemed to be at peace, and it was very hard to realize that we were at war.'

This book is not primarily about the strategy behind the battle, nor the bitter controversies that subsequently raged about who was responsible for winning or losing it. Instead, it focuses on the terrain, and on the way the terrain shaped the battle. The Marne was a vast, sprawling struggle, made up of smaller battles in the various sectors of the front. These component battles had their own, distinct characteristics, partly because they were fought over contrasting landscapes, be it open farmland, or an intricate network of woods and valleys. Many lessons can be learned from seeing these contrasts for yourself, and from following the fighting on the actual ground. Even after a century the battlefield remains largely unspoilt, and yet it lies right on the doorstep of Paris, making it easily accessible to visitors.

Historical overview

When war broke out in August 1914, the Germans launched a massive sweep through Belgium and into northern France, winning the first, great clashes – the Battles of the Frontiers – through superior tactics and an emphasis on seizing the initiative. The British and

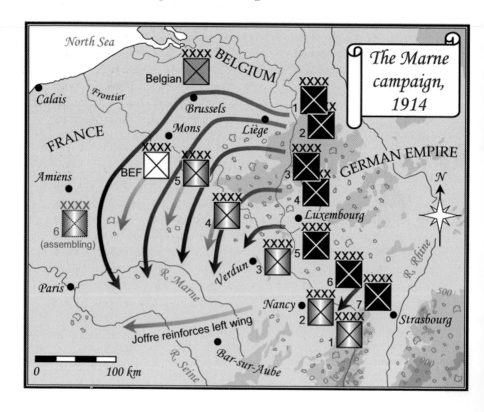

French stumbled back, pivoting on the fortress of Verdun as their weak left wing was driven further and further southwards in an apparently unstoppable retreat. Guns grumbled in the background like the distant roll of a drum, and the night sky took on an ominous, ruddy glow from the burning villages that marked the German advance. 'The awful box up of movements cannot be described,' grumbled a British soldier, Private Pattenden of the 1/Hampshire. 'We have no good officers left, our NCOs are as useless as women, our nerves are all shattered and we don't know what the end will be. Death is on every side and to meet it I am not afraid, because it will all be ended then. No one can describe how one feels, it is an empty void in oneself and care is forgotten. To get away from the guns is our effort and to do this one must walk, walk hard, hour on hour . . .'.

The French commander-in-chief, *Général de division* Joseph Joffre, kept his nerve despite the scale of the crisis that confronted him. As early as 25 August he issued a plan, which, although progressively modified, would provide the basis for victory on the Marne a fortnight later. The key element was the formation of a new force – soon designated the *6e armée* – outside the path of the oncoming German armies, and in a position to strike into their western flank. To help create this additional army, Joffre shifted corps by railway from his right wing, whose position had already stabilized amid the mountains and fortresses of eastern France.

By the beginning of September France still seemed to be on the brink of disaster, and its government left for the safety of Bordeaux in the face of the relentless German advance on Paris. Yet the Germans, too, had suffered heavy losses, and had begun to outrun their supplies. Whereas the British and French were able to replace many of their casualties with fresh troops from their depots, the Germans had to detach units to cover their communications, and to counter a Russian invasion of East Prussia. By the start of the Battle of the Marne, the balance of forces on the all-important western wing had been reversed, with the advantage of numbers now resting with the Allies.

The German Chief of the General Staff, *Generaloberst* Helmuth von Moltke, exerted too loose a grip over the more headstrong of his army commanders. On 31 August his westernmost formation, the *1. Armee* under *Generaloberst* Alexander von Kluck, began to

German infantry march through Brussels, August 1914.

veer south-eastwards in headlong pursuit of the Allies. This new direction took Kluck past the eastern side of Paris, and left his flank exposed. During the first three days of September the potential for a counter-stroke from the capital became obvious to the French high command. Moltke also began to see the possible risk, but failed in his attempts to rein in the *1. Armee*. Kluck ignored his instructions, and continued pressing south-eastwards across the Marne, intent on winning a decisive victory.

By the morning of 4 September the German advance was creating a bulge between the great fortresses of Paris in the west and Verdun 225 km to the east. Joffre planned to thrust against the western flank and rear of this massive salient with the *6e armée*, whilst pinning the Germans down with a general offensive from the south to make it difficult for them to escape. It was a fleeting opportunity, and

Kluck.

required perfect timing. Too soon, and the Germans would not have pressed fully into the trap. Too late, and they might realize their danger and redeploy accordingly.

The key, uncertain element was the British Expeditionary Force (BEF). It was an indispensable part of the proposed counter-offensive, but was not under Joffre's orders. Its commander, Field Marshal Sir John French, had been instructed by his government to co-operate, but as an independent force, and the August disasters had made him cautious, distrustful, and reluctant to incur further losses.

To secure the BEF's participation, Joffre had to resort to appease-
ment, pressure through diplomatic channels, and even emotional
blackmail. On 4 September the French generals on either flank of
the BEF held two separate meetings with senior British officers. At
Melun the military governor of Paris, *Général de division* Joseph
Galliéni, met the Chief of the General Staff, Lieutenant General Sir
Archibald Murray. Meanwhile, at Bray-sur-Seine, 41 km to the east,
the commander of the *5e armée* met Murray's deputy, Major General

Galliéni.

Henry Wilson. The result was two plans for an offensive – broadly similar, but different in key details – and neither of them had yet been approved by Sir John French, who had been absent from both meetings. It was Joffre's responsibility to sort out the confusion, adopt one of these plans, and integrate it into his overall strategy. He had to decide the timing, and confirm the vague British commitment. By the end of 4 September he had issued instructions for a counter-offensive to be launched on the 6th, and the following afternoon he personally visited Sir John French at Melun to quell any lingering doubt that the BEF would take part.

Joffre's offensive duly opened on the 6th – except near Paris, where the battle actually began a day earlier than expected. As the *6e armée* advanced eastwards on the 5th to take up its jumping-off

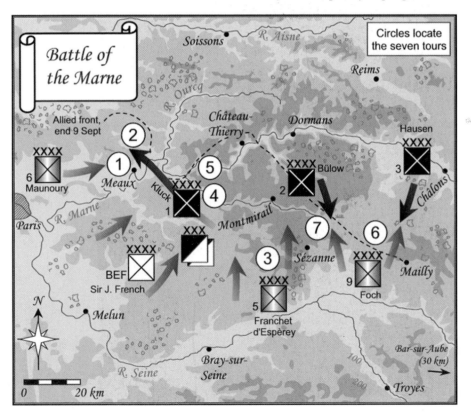

positions near the Ourcq river, it blundered into a German corps covering the *1. Armee*'s rear. This premature action had a crucial effect. Over the next four days Kluck gradually pulled his *1. Armee* back to the north bank of the Marne to confront the *6e armée*. His redeployment changed the whole character of the battle: it foiled French hopes of rolling up the German right wing from the direction of Paris, but created a new vulnerability elsewhere, by opening a gap of 40 km between Kluck and the neighbouring *2. Armee*. The gap was too wide for the two cavalry corps that were screening it to do more than fight delaying actions against the BEF and *5e armée*, whose cautious advance began slowly to prise open the breach.

On the morning of the 8th Moltke sent a representative to the various German armies from his headquarters at Luxembourg, and apparently authorized this staff officer – *Oberstleutnant* Richard Hentsch – to direct his endangered right wing to retreat, should that prove necessary. What Hentsch found was alarming. The widening

Fighting at Sommesous. The Germans took the village from the French **9e armée** *on 8 September.*

gap was making the positions of both the *1.* and *2. Armeen* untenable, and on the morning of the 9th the staff of the latter convinced him that both armies had to fall back to reunite. Later that morning the commander of the *2. Armee* ordered a retirement across the Marne, and towards noon Hentsch reached the headquarters of *1. Armee* and insisted that it also withdraw. The German high command did not immediately realize that this would be anything more than a local and temporary retreat: the movement was not meant to become a wider withdrawal encompassing the other armies further east. But on the 11th, when Moltke finally left Luxembourg to visit his army commanders in person, he found evidence of an increasingly perilous situation, and decided that a general retreat had now become unavoidable.

'Victory, victory!'
Moltke's nerves had broken – he was secretly replaced on the 14th. The oppressively hot weather had also come to an abrupt end. Rain and mud hindered the Allied pursuit, and left a dismal sense of anti-climax. 'It becomes misty', wrote a French gunner, Paul Lintier, on the 10th. 'Under the grey sky, the countryside is dull and monotonous, and weapons, equipment, and corpses still lie about here and there. It wraps us in a dreadful melancholy. We have to repeat to ourselves the words "Victory, victory!" in order to continue experiencing the joy, which nevertheless is so deep, of knowing that the Fatherland has been saved.'

The Germans were able to break contact, and established a continuous front on the commanding heights behind the Aisne river, 40 km north of the Marne. By the end of October the front had extended northwards to the coast, and had solidified all the way from the sea to the Swiss frontier, a distance of some 700 km.

The true cost of the Battle of the Marne will never be known, but in scale it was horrific. Only the BEF, which had advanced into the gap between the German armies, escaped heavy casualties. In fact, few of the British participants were even aware that they were fighting a Battle of the Marne. 'We certainly didn't realize its importance at the time', wrote Arthur Osburn, Medical Officer with the 4th (Royal Irish) Dragoon Guards. 'It seemed but a succession of skirmishes.' Nor did

A huddle of German dead.

Fishing in the Marne. A cartoon published in the French review, l'Illustration, *on 12 September, after the German defeat. 'A barbel?' reads the caption, referring to a type of fish. 'No ... another helmet!'*

ordinary German soldiers grasp that they had suffered a decisive defeat. Time after time during the Battle of the Marne they had demonstrated their tactical superiority in the individual engagements, only to lose the battle as a whole. 'For five days now, the men had been fighting intensely without a break', recalled *Leutnant* Kuhlmann of *Infanterie-Regiment Nr 77*:

> For three days, they had gone without a night's sleep, and had seen no field kitchens, yet their strength was unbroken, and their nerves were like steel. As always, the enemy had once again been overthrown, and in general did not dare to make any large-scale counter-attack. In abandoning the field, we did so with the feeling that we had been victorious, and that we were superior to the French, and we left behind not a single unwounded prisoner.

To explain away their defeat, the Germans ignored the underlying flaws in their command system, and simply sought scapegoats, pinning the blame on Moltke and Hentsch. For many French people, the outcome was just as inexplicable, and they spoke of their deliverance as the 'miracle of the Marne'. Yet to talk of a miracle downplays Joffre's nerve and foresight as a commander, and the courage and self-sacrifice of his troops. The Marne was a victory of generalship, staffwork and morale. It destroyed any illusions of German invincibility and averted a disaster that had threatened France's very existence. Having survived the opening weeks of the war, the Allies could now begin to build up the superior resources that would eventually crush the Central Powers.

Both the duration and the geographical extent of the battle are open to interpretation. According to the French Official History, it lasted from 6 to 9 September, but other accounts include the preliminary clash on the Battlefield of the Ourcq on the 5th, or extend the end of the battle to the 12th. It was not just near Paris that men were killed. Fierce fighting also raged further east, notably around the fortress city of Verdun, and on the heights outside Nancy, and these local battles continued until the 10th or even the 13th. But it was in the west that the situation was most fluid, and it was here more than

German soldiers passing through Brussels, August 1914.

anywhere that the Battle of the Marne was won or lost. The 9th was the crucial day. Thereafter, the outcome was no longer in doubt, and by the morning of the 10th Joffre's left wing had ceased to fight a battle, and had begun a pursuit. This guidebook hence focuses on the western sector, and on the period between 5 and 9 September.

ADVICE FOR TOURERS

In deciding the timing of your visit, remember that some museums are closed during the quieter months of the year, and that ceremonies or re-enactments are generally held around the anniversary of the battle.

The proximity of Paris makes it a feasible base for all except the last and most easterly two tours, which are over 100 km away. But to make the most of your time, you may prefer to stay locally for every tour. Good hotels and restaurants can be found at the following provincial towns and cities, and can be identified using a Michelin guide, an internet search, or a visit to the local tourist information office (page 207):

- Châlons-en-Champagne: 148 km east of Paris. Population 47,000. Suitable base for Tours 6 and 7. Previously known as Châlons-sur-Marne.
- Epernay: 120 km east of Paris. Population 25,000. Suitable base for Tours 6 and 7.
- La Ferté-sous-Jouarre: 58 km east of Paris. Population 9,000. Suitable base for Tours 1, 2, 3, 4 and 5.
- Meaux: 41 km east of Paris. Population 50,000. Suitable base for Tours 1, 2, 3, 4 and 5.
- Sézanne: 103 km east of Paris. Population 5,000. Suitable base for Tours 3, 6 and 7.
- Troyes: 142 km east-south-east of Paris. Population 63,000. Suitable base for Tours 6 and 7.

Be aware that few of the tours pass through large towns, and that shops in remote villages may not be open, if they exist at all. We suggest you take a picnic for your midday meal, and then eat out in the evening at one of the larger towns or cities.

Tours

The tours examine several of the most interesting actions of the Battle of the Marne. Some are tactical studies of the actual fighting, while others take more of a broad overview. They are arranged both in chronological order and, broadly speaking, in geographical sequence from west to east. However, each has been written so it can be understood on its own, so pick just a few should you lack the time to cover them all. Each tour starts with an account of what happened, and then explains what you can see at the key points of interest.

Public transport services are limited in the remoter parts of the countryside, so we advise that you travel around the region by car. The first six tours are designed for driving, but with opportunities to walk around at the various points of interest. Tour 7 is a walking tour, just 7 km long. Boots may prove useful for tracks in wet weather, especially in Tours 1, 6 and 7. The time required to visit the battlefield will depend on how long you want to spend at the museums and viewpoints, but you should allow at least half-a-day for each tour, and up to a full day for Tours 2 and 6. Museum visits are included in Tours 1, 2 and 7, and their contact details are given on page 208, to enable you to obtain up-to-date opening hours.

Length of tours (driving distances):

Tour 1:	15 km	Tour 4:	20 km
Tour 2:	45 km	Tour 5:	35 km
Tour 3:	28 km	Tour 6:	80 km

Maps

To get the most out of your visit, you should obtain some road maps for use in conjunction with this guide, along with a magnetic compass and a pair of binoculars. We recommend the *Top 100 Tourisme et découverte* series, published on a scale of 1:100,000 by the French *Institut géographique national (IGN)*. The following two sheets cover the areas of the tours:

109 (Paris Compiègne)
110 (Reims St-Dizier)

The two sheets to the south may also prove useful:

119 (Evry Melun/Provins)
120 (St-Dizier Chaumont)

The above maps are adequate for navigating your way round the tours in this book. For exploring key sectors you will benefit from the more detailed IGN *Série Bleu* maps, drawn on a scale of 1:25,000. The following are the relevant sheets:

Tour 1: 2513 OT (Meaux/Vallée de l'Ourcq)
Tour 2: 2513 OT (Meaux/Vallée de l'Ourcq); and 2512 OT (Villers-Cotterêts Forêt de Retz)
Tour 3: 2615 E (Esternay)
Tour 4: 2514 E (Coulommiers); and 2614 O (La Fertê-Gaucher)
Tour 5: 2514 E (Coulommiers); and 2513 E (Saâcy-sur-Marne)
Tour 6: 2715 E (Connantre); 2815 O (Fère-Champenoise); 2814 O (Vertus); 2714 E (Montmort-Lucy, marais de St-Gond)
Tour 7: 2714 E (Montmort-Lucy, marais de St-Gond); and 2714 O (Orbais-l'Abbaye)

For exploring Paris, take both a street map of the city centre and a more general map covering the suburbs.

IGN maps can be obtained through the *Institut*'s website (www. ign.fr), or from some map shops in the United Kingdom (try Stanford's, at 12–14 Long Acre, London). In France, you may find them in good, local bookstores. In Paris, visit *Le Monde des cartes*, at 50, *rue de la Verrerie* (near the *Hôtel de ville*, in the *4e arrondissement*).

Copies of the 1:80,000 scale maps used by the BEF in 1914 can be consulted at the National Archives: WO 297/6052 (Sheet 49, 'Meaux'; for Tours 4 and 5, and nearly all of 1 and 2); WO 297/6050 (Sheet 48, 'Paris'; for western edge of Tour 1); WO 297/6040 (Sheet 33, 'Soissons'; for northern edge of Tour 2); WO 297/6063 (Sheet 66, 'Provins'; for Tour 3); WO 297/6054 (Sheet 50, 'Châlons'; for Tour 7, and northern part of Tour 6); and WO 297/6065 (Sheet 67, 'Arcis'; for southern part of Tour 6).

Further research

Suggestions for more detailed background reading can be found on page 201. If you wish to locate the grave of a particular soldier who fell in the war, try the websites listed on page 208.

Times

In 1914 the Germans used Central European Time, and were therefore one hour ahead of the French and British, who were on Western European Time. To avoid confusion, all the times in this book have been standardized to Western European Time. Sunrise during the battle was at 5.16 am (Paris, 6 September). The sun set at 6.21 pm. Civil dawn (the time when it became light enough for objects to be distinguished) was at 4.42 am. Civil twilight was at 6.55 pm.

Road classifications

Bear in mind that the N3 – formerly the main, national road from Paris to Germany – has been reclassified to the east of Meaux as a *route départementale*. Older maps still show the whole road as the N3, but signposts in the *département* of the Seine-et-Marne now refer to the D603, in the Aisne to the D1003, and in the Marne to the D3.

German 77mm gun, knocked out of action.

BATTLEFIELD TOURS

Tour 1

OPENING CLASH

Our first tour examines the preliminary encounter battle on 5 September, when the foremost elements of the *6e armée* ran into a German corps around the villages of Monthyon and Penchard just 40 km north-east of Paris. This was the opening clash of the Battle of the Marne, but was not meant to happen. Joffre had ordered the *6e armée* to be in position to attack eastwards across the Ourcq river on the 6th, the day that he had selected for the start of his counter-offensive. The *6e armée* therefore advanced on the 5th, intending to reach positions north of the city of Meaux, within easy reach of the Ourcq. None of the French commanders, from Joffre down to the regimental officers, expected the *6e armée* to run into German opposition west of the river.

WHAT HAPPENED

Nearly the whole of Kluck's *1. Armee* had already pressed forward across the Marne. But two of its formations – the *IV Reservekorps* and the attached *4. Kavallerie-Division* – were following in its wake, as a flank guard, and were still north of the river. They were moving south, towards the Marne at Meaux, and unknowingly were heading directly across the path of the *6e armée*. Neither of these German formations was at full strength. One-third of the infantry in the *IV Reservekorps* had been detached to cover the lines of communication, while the cavalry division had been badly mauled by the BEF at Néry on 1 September.

General der Artillerie Hans von Gronau, the commander of the *IV Reservekorps*, did not anticipate a battle. Crucially, he had no aircraft attached to his corps, and it was not until mid-morning that he received reports from his cavalry of French troops on the move about 15 km to the west. He then learned that the troops in question

– initially thought to be no more than a cavalry division – were a substantial force of all arms, and that they were marching towards him. Gronau remained unsure just how much of a danger they posed, for his view was blocked by a string of wooded heights known as the *Buttes de la Goële*. They formed a backbone across the land, separating the *plateau du Multien* to the north-east from the *plateau de la Goële* to the south-west, and prevented the two sides from seeing each other as they converged. Only from the top of the hills would Gronau be able to see the situation for himself. Ingrained in him through his years of training was one of the central tenets of German military doctrine: the need to react instantly and vigorously to a threat. An immediate counter-thrust was the only way to blunt the oncoming French advance, and to clarify the situation by securing the vantage points of the hills. At 11.15 am Gronau gave the necessary order, gambling that his boldness in taking the offensive would compensate should he run into a more numerous foe.

By this stage the *IV Reservekorps* had completed its march south-wards for the day, and was looking forward to some rest in its bivouacs some 6–8 km north of Meaux. It now moved off again, switching direction to the west, and the result was a head-on collision with the French on an 8-km front between St-Soupplets in the north, and the villages of Monthyon and Penchard further south. The ground favoured the Germans. Gronau's boldness secured the key features of the battlefield, the twin heights at Monthyon and Penchard. Further west, the ground the French would have to cross was an undulating plateau, cut by a couple of streams, and dotted with a few villages, but otherwise exposed.

From the west came the leading elements of the *6e armée* – two reserve divisions (the *56e* in the north, and the *55e* in the centre), and the *Brigade marocaine* in the south. The French had no warning of the impending clash, for their cavalry reconnaissances failed to detect the German approach. In the centre, the head of the *55e division* had actually halted for a rest at Iverny, just 3 km west of Monthyon, when shells suddenly started bursting around it. French guns riposted against the German batteries that were coming into action around Monthyon, and by 1.30 pm the battle was under way in earnest.

From Monthyon, the string of heights known as the *Buttes de la Goële* curves away towards the town of Dammartin in the north-west,

German infantryman.

forming a spine of hills that marks the northern edge of the battle-field. In this area it was the French who managed to gain the high ground – their *56e division* occupied the wooded ridge of the *Bois des Tillières*, which served as a solid bulwark on this flank. One infantry battalion even managed to occupy the town of St-Soupplets, 1.5 km further north-east, but by 2.00 pm had been evicted and forced back to the heights. Fighting continued in this northern sector for the

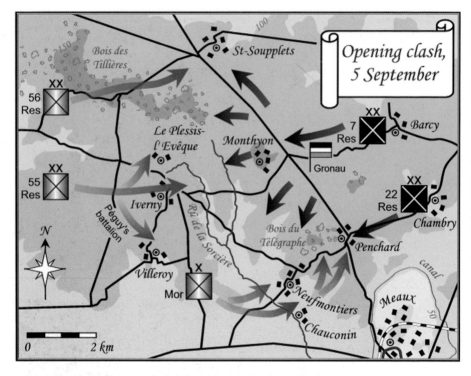

Opening clash, 5 September

Bois des Tillières

St-Soupplets

56 Res

Le Plessis-l'Evêque

Monthyon

7 Res

Gronau

Barcy

55 Res

22 Res

Iverny

Péguy's battalion

N

Rû de la Sorcière

Bois du Télégraphe

Penchard

Chambry

canal

Villeroy

Mor

X

Neufmontiers

Meaux

Chauconin

0   2 km

rest of the day, and the French made several attempts to recapture St-Soupplets.

One of those who witnessed the battle was Mildred Aldrich, a US writer in her early sixties. Her home stood on a hilltop at the village of Huiry, south of the Marne, and gave her a grandstand view across the river. 'The battle had advanced right over the crest of the hill', she wrote. 'The sun was shining brilliantly on silent Mareuil and Chauconin, but Monthyon and Penchard were enveloped in smoke. From the eastern and western extremities of the plain we could see the artillery fire, but owing to the smoke hanging over the crest of the hill on the horizon, it was impossible to get an idea of the positions of the armies.' It was nothing like what she had imagined a battle would be, for she could see no lines of soldiers, or galloping detachments of cavalry. 'Now I was actually seeing a battle, and it was nothing like that. There was only noise, belching smoke, and long drifts of white clouds concealing the hill.'

The most important action flared up on the southern wing at 3.30 pm. Here, the *Brigade marocaine* – Moroccans serving under the French flag – advanced on Penchard from the west. One battalion actually penetrated into the village, only to be thrown out by a decisive counter-attack as Gronau's rearmost units reached the battle-field. Crucially, the Moroccans lacked artillery support, and had become exposed on their northern flank as a result of the *55e division* being pinned down by German fire in front of Monthyon. As the Moroccans broke and poured back to the west, the Germans pursued to the *Rû de la Sorcière*, a stream 2–3 km west of Monthyon and Penchard. But Gronau wisely halted the advance, having realized that he faced a major French offensive.

By dusk the whole plain seemed to be ablaze, from the burning villages and haystacks set alight by the artillery shells. That night the

Moroccans outside Neufmontiers church after the action, searching through captured equipment.

wind changed, and the smoke drifted towards Mildred Aldrich, 9 km away on the opposite side of the Marne, so she could actually smell it. She found it impossible to sleep, as she thought of the soldiers lying dead in the starlight, on such a beautiful night.

For the French, the clash had come as a surprise. They had failed to coordinate their forces or to react sufficiently quickly as the action unfolded; nor was the bulk of the *6e armée* near enough to join the fighting that day and give them a crushing numerical advantage. Only two reserve divisions and the *Brigade marocaine* had actually been engaged, and they had been checked by two depleted German reserve divisions and the remnants of a cavalry division.

Gronau had fulfilled his aim: he was now certain that the French were mounting a serious offensive from the Paris region. But he had taken heavy losses, and knew that his weak corps would be outflanked as more enemy units arrived the next day. To avoid destruction, he fell back under cover of darkness to a new line 7–8 km further north-east, where he would be successively reinforced by other elements of the *1. Armee* as they were recalled from south of the Marne in response to the emerging threat. The French failed to detect Gronau's withdrawal early enough to hamper it; nor did they pursue vigorously. Not until 4.30 am the following day did a company occupy the village of Monthyon, after being pushed forward on reconnaissance.

The fact that the two sides had clashed on the 5th did not cost Joffre the advantage of surprise in the Battle of the Marne as a whole, for it was not immediately clear to the Germans that he was about to launch a general counter-offensive south of the river. But it did rob the *6e armée* of the full impact of its planned thrust into the German flank and rear. Instead of landing a decisive blow, the *6e armée* would be checked during the next four days whilst still trying to reach its intended jumping-off positions.

WHAT TO SEE

The battlefield remains much the same as in 1914, despite the growth of some villages, and the construction of a high-speed railway line that passes through the gap between Monthyon and Penchard. The tour's starting point is Monthyon. To reach it from Meaux, head north-westwards along the N330. When you reach the eastern side of Monthyon, turn left at the crossroads with the D97, and then, immediately afterwards, take the turning to the right. This leads you uphill, and through the town to the church, where you can usually find a parking space.

Point 1: Monthyon

Today Monthyon is a small town of over 1,600 inhabitants, but in 1914 it was just a village with barely more than 700. The church was a German dressing station for the wounded. So, too, was the massive farm of *l'Hôpital* at the southern end of the town (descend the *rue*

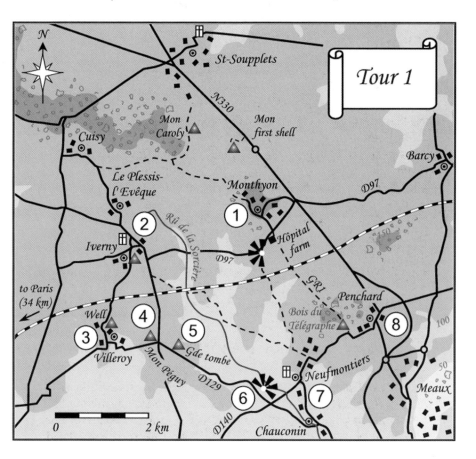

Gambetta from the church, and you will see the farm on the opposite side of the D97).

The hilltop town is screened by trees on its western edge, so to obtain a view over the battlefield you will need to go to the nearby fields. Leave Monthyon by the southern exit, at *l'Hôpital* farm, and turn right on to the D97. After 500 metres, as the D97 bends round to the right, turn off the road and stop on the start of the track that leads off to the left. From here, the view extends westwards all the way to Iverny (2.75 km away), from where the French *55e division* vainly tried to advance across the open terrain. The advantages of the German position are obvious. From their vantage points they could dominate the lower, gently undulating ground to the west.

On the other hand, the French had superior numbers of batteries in this sector. A German staff officer, *Hauptmann* Alfred Wirth, recalled the sheer intensity of their fire. 'Close in front of the village [of Monthyon] was a barn, behind which our staff and a company of infantry were standing under cover, but even this point was pounded with shells in no time at all. We had to leave this hell for the rear, while the infantry deployed and slowly advanced.'

At the point where you are standing, three batteries of the *Reserve-Feldartillerie-Regiment Nr 7* were smashed by the French artillery. The 77mm guns were silenced one after the other, and as many as fifty-three officers and men were killed. Artillery normally took up covered positions, hidden from view behind a hill, where they were more difficult for enemy batteries to locate. But the nature of the encounter battle meant that the German batteries had suddenly come into action as they advanced along the D97. Once the battle had begun, the gunners soon found themselves too heavily engaged to withdraw from their dangerously exposed position. Eventually, the survivors simply huddled closely together behind the meagre protection of their gun shields, abandoning any attempt to return fire.

Point 2: Iverny
We shall now go and see the battlefield from the French side. Drive westwards along the D97. After 1.5 km you descend into the valley of the *Rû de la Sorcière*, which marked the limit reached by the German counter-attack that evening. (The stream itself has been canalized, and so follows a slightly different course than before.)

After another 700 metres, just east of Iverny, you approach a T-junction with the D27. Go right, and drive straight through the outskirts of Iverny, ignoring the roads that turn off to the left, until you see the local war memorial. As well as commemorating Iverny's own dead, the monument honours those French soldiers whose bodies were found locally after the battle. The nine who were identified include *Capitaine* Joseph Michel of the *246e régiment*, who was killed by a shrapnel ball while standing among his men to set an example of fearlessness. 'His death deeply affected me,' wrote a fellow officer, 'for he was likeable, and popular with everyone. His men trusted him completely.' *Capitaine* Michel's son, René, later wrote a detailed book about the *55e division* in this action, and dedicated it to his memory. Also listed on the monument is *Lieutenant* Adolphe Whitcomb, a staff officer who was sent to summon reinforcements after the action began, only to be killed by shrapnel on the way. As a result, the *246e régiment* was left to bear the full weight of the action at Iverny until the evening.

Continue another 150 metres along the D27 to the local cemetery on the left-hand side of the road, just beyond the exit from Iverny. *Lieutenant* Whitcomb is among the soldiers buried here – under the tall, imposing monument on the left of the entrance path.

Return along the D27, and take the first right, the *rue du Tillet*, which leads you into the centre of Iverny. After exploring the village, leave along the *rue du Fresne* (you can join this street 50 metres east of the church). As you pass house number 25 *bis*, on the left, pause at the roadside monument. Dedicated to the heroes of the Marne, it remembers the action at Iverny, and is inscribed with an extract from Joffre's order of the day, issued on 6 September (page 193).

Continue along the *rue du Fresne* as it emerges from the southern side of Iverny, and head across the countryside to Villeroy. Pass over the high-speed railway line, and then, as you approach Villeroy, note the old, stone well standing isolated in the fields 100 metres to your left. This is a key relic, because of its connection with one of the heroes of the battle, *Lieutenant* Charles Péguy of the *276e régiment*. Péguy's battalion was moved forward in the afternoon to cover the southern flank of the rest of the *55e division*, and to fill the gap between the division and the *Brigade marocaine*. By 3.00 pm the battalion had reached the northern exit of Villeroy, and, since it was

Lieutenant *Whitcomb's monument in Iverny cemetery.*

so hot, Péguy's men had a drink from the well. An hour and a half later the battalion went into action east of Villeroy, and we will discover its fate after we pass through the village.

Point 3: Villeroy

Villeroy contains a fascinating little museum run by a local resident, Jacques Braquet. You will find it near the church, at 1, *rue Charles Péguy*. Exhibits include dioramas, a range of relics excavated from various battlefields, and even Péguy's *képi* and epaulettes (not those he wore during the battle). You are advised to contact the museum before travelling to the battlefield, in order to arrange a visit (page 208). After exploring Villeroy, drive along the *rue Charles Péguy* (the D129), and follow it round, out of the village, and then along the superb avenue of trees, sloping gently up to the crossroads with the D27.

Point 4: Péguy's monument

At the crossroads you will find a tall, roughly hewn stone cross, with an inscription explaining that Péguy was killed in the nearby fields. When the war broke out, Péguy was mobilized as a reservist officer. He was 41 years old, married with three children, and with a fourth on the way. Passionate and idealistic, he was keen to make his mark as a writer, and to further the cause of social justice, and since 1900 had been publishing his work in a literary review he had founded under the title of the *Cahiers de la quinzaine*.

His career had seen only modest success. He was a tempestuous man, torn between his Catholic faith and his socialist views. War brought release from his inner torment, and he joined his regiment happy at having had the opportunity to bid farewell to his family and friends, and to forgive past quarrels. He was confident of victory, and hopeful that it would

Péguy.

Péguy's monument.

lead to a general disarmament. 'If I do not return, remember me without any grief', he wrote to his wife. 'Thirty years of life would be worth less than what we are going to do in a matter of weeks.'

Péguy's nickname in the army was *le pion* ('the beak'), for he seemed so similar to a little provincial schoolmaster – a bit strict, perhaps, yet also warm-hearted and conscientious. During a march he looked like a sheepdog as he went up and down his company's column with words of encouragement. One of the soldiers paid him the ultimate tribute. 'For a *lieutenant*', the man remarked, 'you're a decent sort.'

Towards 4.30 pm Péguy's battalion was ordered to advance east-wards from the northern exit of Villeroy. Its mission was to support the *Brigade marocaine*, which was attacking Penchard. Towards 4.45 pm the battalion reached the road that ran south from Iverny (the D27), beyond which the ground was swept by bullets. By now, the *Brigade marocaine* was pouring back after being repulsed. A staff officer arrived to urge the battalion forward to cover the Moroccans' retreat. The battalion tried to advance, but came under a murderous fire. Péguy told his section to lie down, but he himself remained standing, and was shot in the head, in the fields north-east of his monument. The remnants of his battalion were crushed and thrown back on Villeroy as the Germans attacked from the east.

One of the stone blocks on Péguy's monument bears an orientation table, and extracts from a poem that he had published less than a year before the war, under the title *Eve*. The verses have become famous, not least as they seem to anticipate his death:

> *Happy those who have died in the epic battles,*
> *lying on the ground with their face looking up at God …*
> *Happy those who have died for their hearth and fire,*
> *and the poor honours of their ancestral house.*
>
> *Happy those who have died, for they have returned*
> *into the primordial clay and earth.*
> *Happy those who have died in a just war.*
> *Happy the ripe ears of corn, the harvested wheat.*

Péguy has been acclaimed as one of the great French writers of his age, but the irony of his work is that he became famous only after his death – and, indeed, precisely because of the circumstances in which he died. During his lifetime he had not been widely known. It was the war that transformed him into a great, symbolic figure, for he fell while repelling the Germans in the action that marked the high point of their advance – no other engagement of the entire war was fought so close to Paris. Péguy gave his life for his country, as had his heroine, Joan of Arc, and his self-sacrifice gave his work a resonance that had hitherto been absent. He became a national icon, and also a unifying figure. His personal upheavals as he searched for an identity during the pre-war years reflected some of France's own soul-searching, and he symbolized the *Union sacrée*, the setting-aside of political quarrels for the sake of the war effort, for he managed to unite the two sides of France – the Catholicism and patriotism of the Right, and the social idealism of the Left.

Behind the sentiments that Péguy expressed in *Eve* lies a further irony, for had he not been killed at the start of the war, he would probably have grown disillusioned. 'The war had lit up, calmed, and given serenity to his tormented soul', noted one of his contemporaries, the writer Romain Rolland. 'It did him good. If he had survived, I fear that he would have suffered years of bitterness.'

Point 5: *La Grande tombe*
Continue 500 metres along the D129, and then stop at the *Nécropole nationale de la Grande tombe*. This is a mass grave, containing the remains of 133 French soldiers, one-quarter of whom are unknown. The grave was created at the time of the battle, but the monument, with its colourful mosaic, was added in 1932.

In previous wars within Europe, almost all the dead were cremated or buried in mass graves. By the time of the First World War it was more common for soldiers of all ranks to have individual graves, yet mass burials often proved necessary in the opening weeks because the front lines had not yet become static, and because such large numbers of bodies had to be buried quickly before they decomposed in the heat.

Among the names listed on the monument, note those of the officers on the top line. Among them is Péguy, and it was partly because of his presence that this particular grave became a focal point for commemorations. The other officers buried here include Péguy's company commander, *Capitaine* Pierre Guérin, and a comrade, *Lieutenant* Charles de la Cornillière. By the end of the day the company was left with just one of its four officers, and that surviving officer would be mortally wounded a week later.

Point 6: Moroccan viewpoint

Drive further along the D129. You are following the route taken by the *Brigade marocaine* as it advanced during the early afternoon. After covering 2 km from the *Grande tombe*, you will see a triangular sign indicating an approaching crossroads. Stop at the roadside about 50 metres before this sign – be careful of the ditch. From here, you have a superb, panoramic view of the scene of the Moroccans' attack.

The view from Point 6.

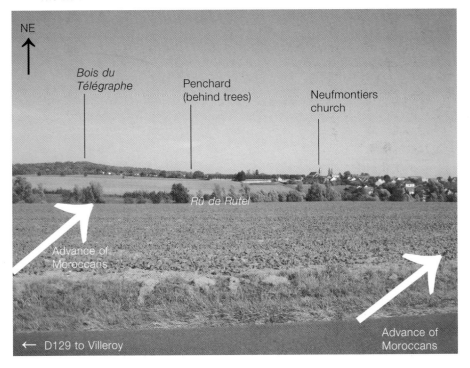

Morocco had been a French protectorate since 1912, and units of Moroccan auxiliaries had been organized to help pacify the country. The two infantry regiments of the *Brigade marocaine* consisted of hardened soldiers, and were commanded partly by French officers, including 25-year-old *Lieutenant* Alphonse Juin, who would be made a *maréchal* in 1952 after his service in the Second World War.

The leading regiment of the *Brigade marocaine* passed through Villeroy at around 12.30 pm, and pressed on eastwards in the belief that the way ahead was clear. But the regiment came under heavy artillery fire as it approached the valley of the *Rû de Rutel* (a continuation of the *Rû de la Sorcière*), and was stopped on the far side of the valley by German infantry fire from the *Bois du Télégraphe*, the wooded hill on the western side of Penchard.

To resume the stalled attack, the rest of the brigade was now committed. One of its battalions, under *Capitaine* Jacques de Richard d'Ivry, slipped to the right, around the village of Neufmontiers, in order to extend the attack, and to turn the German flank. Moving across the fields, it reached Penchard at 3.30 pm, only to be flung back by a vigorous German counter-attack.

Point 7: Neufmontiers

We will now go forwards to see where d'Ivry's battalion was engaged. From the viewpoint, continue to the crossroads with the D140, and turn left for Neufmontiers. The road dips, climbs again into the village, and arrives at the green by the church. Stop here to look around. The local war memorial on the eastern side of the green pays tribute to the soldiers who fell on 5 September, and explains that this was where they checked the German onrush towards Paris.

When *Capitaine* d'Ivry's battalion was thrown back from Penchard, three Moroccan companies made a brief stand at Neufmontiers to try to cover their retreat, but at 4.20 pm they, too, were ordered to fall back. The Germans occupied the village by dusk, but abandoned it that night, leaving behind some of their wounded in the church, which was a dressing station. The French returned to Neufmontiers on the morning of the 6th. If you go into the church today, you can still see some remarkable graffiti on the walls – pleas scrawled by the wounded and now preserved under pieces of glass. The church is usually closed except for services, but to gain entry you can ask

Inside Neufmontiers church today.

Graffiti on the church walls.

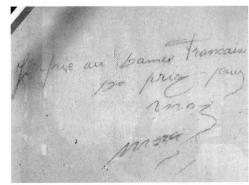

Wounded soldiers in the church.

Neufmontiers cemetery. **Capitaine** *d'Ivry's grave is in the middle.*

at the *mairie*, which you will find 50 metres to the south-east (check on the *mairie*'s opening hours when planning your tour).

You will also want to visit the local cemetery. Walk 75 metres along the side road from the north-western side of the church, and then turn left, past the tennis courts, and you will come to the cemetery on your left. Just inside the entrance is buried *Capitaine* d'Ivry, who died during the clash at Penchard. He had insisted on being placed back on his horse after he had twice been wounded, and he was then shot

Capitaine *d'Ivry.*

once more. His body was found next day with nine bullet holes. To the left lies one of his officers, *Sous-lieutenant* Emile-Maurice Poyelle, who was killed while firing his revolver at the Germans around him.

Now drive to Penchard for the final stop of the tour. From Neufmontiers church, follow the D140 as it winds its way through the village and out into the countryside. The wooded hill on the left is the *Bois du Télégraphe*. It was so named because a semaphore telegraph tower used to stand on the summit, one of a chain of posts between Paris and Strasbourg. Note the tall stone cross standing at the edge of the wood, 100 metres on your left, just before the D140 bends to the right. This marks the grave of *Capitaine* Guy Hugot-Derville, which we will visit after parking in Penchard.

Point 8: Penchard

In 1914 Penchard had just half as many inhabitants as Monthyon, its neighbour 3 km to the north-west. Whereas Monthyon stands on a hill-top, Penchard occupies the south-eastern slopes of the *Bois du Télégraphe*.

It was 3.30 pm when *Capitaine* d'Ivry's battalion of Moroccans reached the southern edge of the *Bois du Télégraphe* and the village of Penchard. For Gronau, it was a dangerous situation, as the Moroccans were on the verge not only of gaining the vantage point of the hill, but of making his entire position untenable by turning his flank.

To win time, the German artillery contained the Moroccans inside Penchard, setting the village on fire. Then, towards 4.00 pm, a German infantry brigade reached the scene and launched a devastating counter-attack. Fierce fighting raged in the village streets and amid the dense undergrowth of the *Bois du Télégraphe*. The outnumbered Moroccans were thrown back, and poured out of the wood to the west, where they had to run a gauntlet of fire from a *Jäger* battalion that had outflanked them by going round the northern side of the hill.

The rest of the *Brigade marocaine* also gave way in the face of the counter-attack. Such was the vigour of the pursuit that some German infantrymen penetrated to within 1 km of Villeroy. The *Brigade marocaine* lost nineteen officers and 1,150 men killed or wounded that day, and *Lieutenant* Juin was forthright about the costly failure. 'It was becoming clear that in the rest of this war we were going to have to adapt,' he wrote.

You will find the church at Penchard on the northern side of the D140, along the *rue de l'Eglise*, which leads uphill past the right-hand side of the *mairie*. Enter the adjoining cemetery through the smaller of the gates (not the large gate for vehicles), and just inside on your left you will find a mass grave of forty-one German soldiers. In fact, they died not in the Battle of the Marne but four decades earlier, during the war of 1870–1.

From here, you can explore the *Bois du Télégraphe* on foot. Previously a military terrain, it has now been opened to the public, except for some dangerous areas that were formerly used for quarrying. Several access points exist, including one up the road past the church. You will see how easily an attacking unit could become swallowed up in the woodland, and lose its cohesion and sense of direction.

While you are in the *Bois du Télégraphe*, you will want to visit the grave of *Capitaine* Hugot-Derville, which you passed as you drove towards Penchard. He was a company commander in *Capitaine* d'Ivry's battalion, and was wounded and unhorsed during the attack. Unable to retreat, he remained behind to fight on with his revolver, and his body was found next morning on the hill. He had expressed the wish, in the event of his death, to be buried where he fell, and so his family, instead of bringing his body home, erected this granite cross, which also commemorates his two brothers who died in the war. To reach it, go to the point where the GR1 footpath reaches the D140 at the southern edge of the wood. Then walk back up the footpath for 150 metres, until you see a narrow path sloping downhill on your left. This leads you through the wood to the rear of the cross.

Optional visit

If time permits, make an excursion to St-Soupplets, 7 km away on the northern edge of the fighting zone. Your first stop lies midway between Monthyon and St-Soupplets. As you drive north-westwards along the N330, you pass a roundabout at the northern outskirts of Monthyon (the turning on the right leads to Fescheux). Continue another 350 metres along the N330, up the hill, to where the road bends to the left, and then turn left on to a track. At the time of writing, the track is immediately in front of a ruined, red-brick house. It is untarmacked, though practicable for vehicles, and may

Monument to **Capitaine** *Hugot-Derville.*

be blocked by a sign reading *Chantier interdit au public* ('no public access'). The track winds up a slight hill for 500 metres, to a final bend, just before it reaches a gate at a quarry entrance. Here, you will see a monument on your left, marking the point from which the first artillery shot of the action is thought to have been fired. 'From this place', reads the inscription, 'a German 77mm gun fired the first shell at 12.30 pm on 5 September 1914, marking the start of the Battle of the Marne.' The Germans reached this point as they pushed westwards to encounter the French. Two guns of *Reserve-Feldartillerie-Regiment Nr 7* galloped up, and opened fire on some French infantry and artillery near Le Plessis-l'Evêque, barely 3 km to the south-west. Another three batteries of the same artillery regiment soon became involved in a separate artillery duel on the southern side of Monthyon, at the location we visited under Point 1. The exact time of the first shell is uncertain – it may well have been half-an-hour later than stated on the monument.

Return to the N330 and continue into the centre of St-Soupplets. Have a look at the local war memorial in the courtyard of the *mairie* (200 metres east of the church). On one side it lists its own fallen sons, while on the other are inscribed the names of the soldiers of the *6e armée* who were killed during the fighting around St-Soupplets. Incredibly, one name – that of Henri Caroly – qualifies to appear on both sides of the monument. He was not only a local man, being the son of the owner of the *Château de Maulny* (now the *mairie*), but also one of the soldiers killed here on 5 September, while serving in the *276e régiment*. By sheer coincidence, he had ended up in action just 2 km from his father's home, and since he knew the local area, he was acting as a guide for his company when he was killed. (He was in a different battalion from Péguy, and hence fought in a different sector of the battlefield.)

Caroly now lies in the cemetery of St-Soupplets, 200 metres north of the *mairie*, in his family's tomb (Grave number B08 218). You may also want to see his initial grave, erected where he fell outside the town. While on your way there, visit the *rue du 5 septembre 1914* (near the *Carrefour* supermarket, on the western side of the N330), where you will find a monument commemorating the French soldiers who fell at St-Soupplets. Then head 250 metres south-eastwards along the N330, turn right on to the *rue du Sauvoy*, then left into the *avenue du Montboulon.* At the roundabout, take the *rue de la Bizière.* After 200 metres, at the bend in the road, you will see a path leading off to the right. Walk 600 metres along this path, keeping the fence on your left, until you come to Caroly's monument.

Caroly's monument, where he fell.

Tour 2

BATTLE OF THE OURCQ

The events of 5 September were a mere curtain-raiser for the fighting that raged in the *6e armée*'s sector for another four days, growing steadily in scale as it sucked in more and more reinforcements. This great clash north of the Marne is known as the Battle of the Ourcq, taking its name from a tributary of the river. Since the tour is longer than the one before, and covers an area four times as large, we shall focus on the main points of interest, so as to gain a general overview of the battle and of the nature of the terrain over which it was fought.

WHAT HAPPENED

Despite having blunted the *6e armée*'s offensive on the 5th, Gronau knew that he was too outnumbered to hold his existing positions. During the night he therefore withdrew his *IV Reservekorps* to a new position 7–8 km further north-east. He was now in the middle of the *plateau du Multien*, a vast, fertile area of farmland. Gently undulating, and largely devoid of trees, it commands broad vistas, bounded by forests to the north, the Ourcq valley to the east, and the rugged spine of the *Buttes de la Goële* to the south-west. The openness of this terrain left attacking units badly exposed, not only to artillery but also to rifles and machine-guns, for most of the crops had been harvested, creating superb fields of fire. The only major towns – notably Meaux, Dammartin and Nanteuil-le-Haudouin – lay at the edges of the plateau, where they were linked by the railway lines and the great *chaussées*. The 400 square km of ground in the middle were studded with villages and large farms, all of which offered potential strongpoints.

Three tributaries of the Ourcq cut through this great plateau: the Thérouanne in the south, the Gergogne in the centre, and the

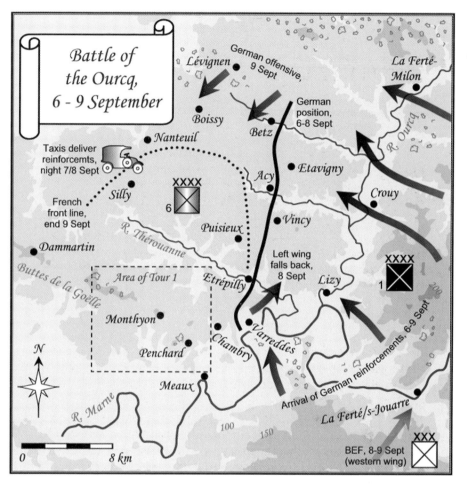

Battle of
the Ourcq,
6 - 9 September

German offensive,
9 Sept

La Ferté-
Milon

Lévignen

German
position,
6-8 Sept

Boissy

Betz

Nanteuil

Taxis deliver
reinforcemts,
night 7/8 Sept

Acy

Etavigny

Crouy

XXXX
6

French
front line,
end 9 Sept

Silly

R. Thérouanne

Puisieux

Vincy

Dammartin

Left wing
falls back,
8 Sept

Lizy

XXXX
1

Buttes de la Goële

Area of Tour 1

Etrépilly

Monthyon

Varreddes

Chambry

Arrival of German reinforcements, 6-9 Sept

Penchard

N

Meaux

R. Marne

100

150

La Ferté/s-Jouarre

0   8 km

BEF, 8-9 Sept
(western wing)

XXX

Grivette in the north. These partly wooded valleys passed at right-angles through the front lines, and the villages nestling inside them, such as Acy and Etrépilly, saw especially bitter fighting.

Gronau's position lay 8 km west of the Ourcq and parallel to it, and covered enough ground for reinforcements to deploy after crossing the river behind him. His southern flank rested securely on the Marne at Varreddes, but the northern wing at Vincy was vulnerable to being turned. As the battle progressed, the front extended further and further north as both sides tried to outflank their opponent.

Endless marching

It was late in the evening of 5 September before news of the unexpected clash at Monthyon reached Kluck, the commander of the *1. Armee*. He was still unsure whether the French attack on the *IV Reservekorps* was more than a diversionary thrust. His advance had carried his other corps up to 40 km south of the Marne, but as the seriousness of the situation grew clear over the next two days, he successively ordered them back across the river to join Gronau.

The march of Kluck's men to the Ourcq constituted one of the most remarkable feats of the battle. Units already exhausted by the 600-km sweep through Belgium and northern France now had to change direction and cover another 50 or 80 km to the Ourcq, with little rest and often through much of the night, only to go into action on their arrival. The exhausted soldiers marched mechanically, dozing as they did so, and every sudden halt caused them to blunder nose-first into the cooking pots of the men in front. *Oberleutnant* Cordt von Brandis of *Infanterie-Regiment Nr 24* described weary columns of men limping through the town of La Ferté-Milon, and remembered it as one of the most demoralizing moments of the whole war. But then one of the soldiers picked up a drum lying on the road. Another found a trumpet, and between them they began playing *O Deutschland, hoch in Ehren*. The effect was electrifying. The men immediately closed up their ranks, and defiantly sang the words as they tramped on with renewed vigour towards the booming of the guns. 'That', added Brandis, 'was the spirit of 1914.'

Suffocating heat

The *6e armée* had the advantage of numbers, but by too small a margin to secure victory. It was a composite force, uneven in quality, and hastily cobbled together using reserve divisions, units withdrawn from North Africa, and formations that Joffre had transferred from the more easterly armies. Not all of these disparate elements were available at the start of the battle, and instead had to be committed as they arrived.

'The struggle extended all around us, from one horizon to the other,' wrote a French dragoon, 'and if it was incomprehensible to our officers it was still more so to us private soldiers.... The heat was suffocating. The exhausted men, covered with a layer of black

French troops in action during the Battle of the Ourcq.

dust adherent from sweat, looked like devils. ... The air was burning; thirst was intolerable, and there was no possibility of procuring a drop of water. All around us the guns thundered. The horizon was, as it were, encircled with a moving line of bursting shells, and we knew nothing, absolutely nothing.'

Over the entire area hung the sickly smell of decomposing bodies. Roads to the rear tended to be congested with vehicles and wounded men, yet out in front stretched expanses of terrain that often seemed almost empty, with no troops visible except some skirmishers, since the reserves were waiting out of sight until required. Occasionally, battalions might be seen attacking as if in an old battle painting, with flags flying, but for much of the time it was merely artillery fire and burning villages that indicated the progress of the action. 'The battlefield looked as if it had died out', wrote a German staff officer, *Hauptmann* Alfred Wirth. 'The long infantry lines were nowhere to be seen, and the artillery, too, had sought positions that hid them from sight. Only the clouds of smoke from bursting shots, and the continuous roaring, crashing, howling, and whistling proclaimed that a fierce battle was under way here.'

Race against time

Kluck intended to hold on until he had built up enough strength to launch a powerful offensive in the north, in order to crush the *6e armée* by falling on its flank. Throughout 7 and 8 September the battle continued indecisively, with attacks on both sides making only limited and temporary gains. The climax came on the 9th. By now, after four days spent attacking, the *6e armée* was reduced to the defensive, and its outlook was grim. 'Extreme weariness everywhere', noted Galliéni after visiting its headquarters on the afternoon of the 8th. That evening, he ordered its commander, *Général de division* Joseph Maunoury, to hold on until the BEF's advance to the Marne further east could take effect. 'It is therefore essential that you hold your positions tomorrow, by hanging on to the ground to the last of your strength.'

The *6e armée* still had a limited numerical superiority overall, but not in the crucial northern sector, where Kluck was planning to attack. Too many of Maunoury's divisions were in the south, and, having expended themselves during the previous four days, had little remaining combat value. In the north, by contrast, just three French divisions had to face an offensive by five German ones.

But Kluck was running out of time. His offensive was delayed, largely because the newly arrived *IX Armeekorps* was simply too exhausted to advance until after 11.00 am. By then, the whole objective had changed, for Kluck had become alarmed by the situation in his rear, where the BEF was now crossing the Marne. His attack in the north, having hitherto been intended as a decisive onslaught, now had the less ambitious aim of distracting the French and covering a withdrawal of his endangered left wing. In fact, rather than gaining ground overall, the entire *1. Armee* was simply beginning to rotate anti-clockwise, so it would face south instead of west.

Kluck's northern wing had to advance some 6 km before it came up against the French position, and so it progressed easily at first. But thereafter it encountered increasing resistance, and at 5.00 pm, after taking the villages of Boissy and Fresnoy, it found itself checked by artillery fire. The plain ahead was so exposed that any further advance was impossible. In any case, orders to halt the offensive had already been issued, for Kluck's situation had grown so precarious that only a general retreat could save his army from disaster. Suddenly, the battle was over. 'In the evening, the gunfire ceased', noted a French soldier, *Caporal* Henri Bury, 'and it was so calm that you would have thought you were at manoeuvres.'

Despite being outclassed by the Germans tactically, the *6e armée* had made a crucial contribution to the victory of the Marne. In five days of fighting it had absorbed the whole of Kluck's *1. Armee*, thereby unbalancing the German western wing, and opening the way across the Marne for the BEF and the *5e armée*, whose advance we shall follow in the three subsequent tours.

WHAT TO SEE

The tour starts at the city of Meaux. You can easily reach it from Paris by driving eastwards along the N3. (The statue of *Maréchal* Galliéni, which used to stand at the southern side of this road, 7 km west of Meaux, has been removed, leaving just the pedestal.) The city centre has a limited amount of car-parking. If you are unable to find a space at the railway station, then try along the *boulevard Jean Rose* on the northern side of the ramparts, or at the central car-park on the *quai Jacques Prévert*. Failing that, cross the Marne to the *Marché* quarter on the south bank.

Point 1: Meaux

Lying on a loop of the Marne, Meaux is a bustling city of 50,000 inhabitants. Back in 1914 it had little more than a quarter of that number, but was militarily important as a major road-hub just 40 km from the centre of Paris. Over 85 per cent of the population fled in the face of the German advance, but in the event the city escaped serious destruction despite some shelling. Nor did it have to undergo the rigours of occupation, for the only German forces to enter it were some reconnaissance patrols.

The old city is clustered around the *Cathédrale St-Etienne* on the north side of the Marne. Inside the cathedral, on its southern wall, is a plaque dedicated to the memory of the one million dead of the

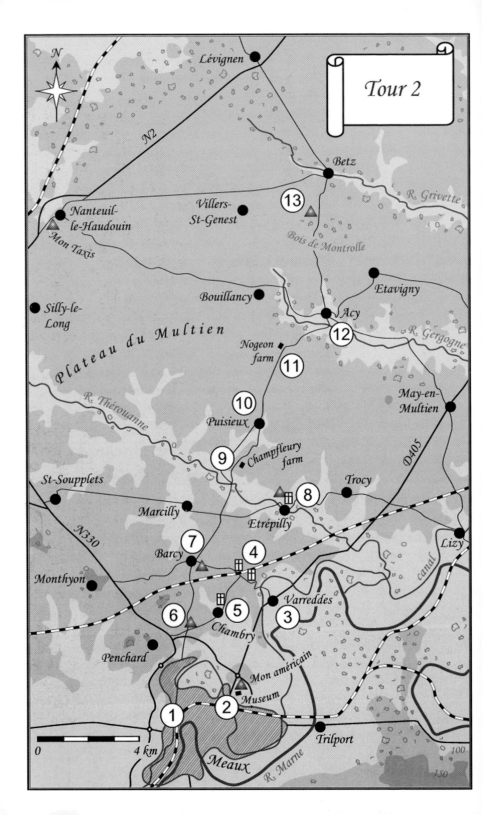

Meaux: the **pont du Marché** *in 1914.*

The imperfectly repaired bridge today.

British Empire who fell in the First World War. Another plaque lists the Bishops of Meaux, including *Monseigneur* Emmanuel Marbeau, who held the post from 1910 until his death in 1921. An inspirational figure, he was among the few civilians to remain at Meaux during the battle, and became its figurehead, helping to organize the running of the paralysed city in the absence of the authorities. During that time wounded soldiers began arriving, and had to be cared for despite the limited resources. Afterwards, Marbeau played a leading role in the annual commemorations of the victory, for which Meaux was the focal point.

The old bridge over the Marne – the *pont du Marché* – used to be lined on its western side with water-mills, but they were destroyed by a fire in June 1920. One of the arches, near the north bank, was blown up on 3 September 1914 when the BEF passed through the city during the retreat from Mons, and if you look carefully you will see that this arch has never been properly repaired.

Point 2: *Musée de la Grande guerre*

The Battlefield of the Ourcq lies to the north of Meaux, but you should first visit the *Musée de la Grande guerre* in the city's outskirts. This important museum opened in 2011, and is devoted to the war as a whole. It is not marked on older maps, but can be found 3.5 km north-east of the city centre, and is well signposted. To reach it, take the D405 out of Meaux, heading in the direction of Soissons. The museum is on the right, near the top of the hill, and has both a car-park and a café. Allow two to three hours for exploring its remarkable collection of relics.

Next to the museum, the massive *Monument américain* is a tribute to the French soldiers who fought at the Marne, and a symbol of American friendship. In the United States the battle came to be seen as a victory not just for France – a fellow republic – but for freedom, civilization and the right to be free from the fear of invasion. The idea of the memorial was conceived in 1916, even before the United States entered the war. The anniversary of the Marne was already being linked with the birthday, on 6 September 1757, of the *marquis* de Lafayette, the French soldier who had helped the Americans win their independence from Britain. The monument was to be a gift to

Monument américain.

France from the US people, in return for the Statue of Liberty, which had been given to the United States and unveiled in 1886.

The design was revised several times by the sculptor, Frederick MacMonnies. His original sketch showed a winged figure brandishing a standard in the air, but this became Joan of Arc in armour, and then the anguished yet defiant woman you see today. Carved from limestone, it depicts a mother – representing both France and Liberty – weeping over the body of her dead son. The model for the figure was MacMonnies' sister-in-law, Marion Jones Farquhar, who won fame in her own right as a tennis champion (in 1900 she became the first US woman to play at Wimbledon).

MacMonnies himself had spent much of his adult life living and working in France. He had been in Paris at the time of the battle, and, although too old to fight as a volunteer, did what he could to help the French war effort. He hence felt an intense, personal connection with his project. 'Never before have I undertaken anything with such deep feeling', he explained to *The New York Times* in 1917. 'I was on the battlefield of the Marne itself while it was still warm from the tremendous struggle. The reality of it – I could still hear the cannon booming away in the distance – I carry as an ineffaceable impression.'

The monument was finally unveiled on 11 September 1932. Its location is deeply symbolic, for it overlooks the Marne valley and marks the area where the Germans were checked – the southern end of their position during the Battle of the Ourcq lay just 3 km to the north-east, outside Varreddes.

Point 3: Varreddes

Retrieve your car, rejoin the D405 and head north-eastwards away from Meaux. At the roundabout continue in the same direction along the D405 to Varreddes. When you reach the town centre, stop at the little car-park beside the *mairie*.

This low-lying town marked the southern end of the 1. *Armee*'s position. The Germans in this area ended up defending a dangerously exposed salient, perched precariously on the semi-circular rim of high ground west of Varreddes. They came under intense artillery fire, which was directed inwards because of the concentric nature of the front line. A company commander, *Leutnant* Jordan of *Grenadier-*

Wounded German soldiers at the **mairie** *of Varreddes. The Germans used the building as a dressing station.*

Varreddes: the **mairie** *today.*

Regiment Nr 2, described how his men had to work their way forwards on all fours when ordered to reinforce the front line south-west of the town. 'The *chaussée* was cratered by direct hits, the trees felled, and the ditches filled with dead and wounded. The enemy artillery fire increased to an intensity previously thought to be impossible.... The hours that followed have never been forgotten by those who lived through them, and even today are known all too accurately as the hell of Varreddes.'

It is easy to sympathize with what the German soldiers had to endure – until you examine the war memorial plaque on the front of the *mairie*. The list of civilian victims near the bottom is a reminder that the Marne was not merely a victory but a liberation. Although most of the population of Varreddes had fled before the German arrival, some remained even during the battle. On 8 September the *1. Armee* finally abandoned the town as it pulled its southern wing back to a stronger position. Nearly twenty male inhabitants were taken away as hostages, and were forced to walk, even though most of them were in their sixties or seventies. Several were murdered when they became too exhausted to continue, and it was 1915 before the survivors returned from Germany.

Point 4: The military cemeteries

Leave Varreddes along the D97, which runs north-westwards from near the *mairie*. (The turning is signposted for Chambry.) The road crosses the tree-lined Ourcq canal, and then winds its way up the wooded slopes of the valley before emerging on to the open plateau. Continue another 200 metres, and stop at the cluster of trees on the right. This is the German military cemetery, and it marks Kluck's front line on the rim of high ground above the Varreddes hollow. Over 1,000 dead are buried here, with more than nine-tenths of them in a mass grave. Just sixty-eight are buried separately, with either a cross of their own, or one shared with a comrade.

The nearby French cemetery offers an interesting comparison. It lies 400 metres to the north-west, on the right of the road, and immediately beyond the bridge over the high-speed railway line. (You will find parking and a picnic area alongside.) The design is broadly similar, with mass graves at the back and individual ones in front, but the focal point is the tricolour flag. The number of dead buried here is only slightly more – over 1,300 – but the cemetery is noticeably larger in area than its German counterpart, and more than one-quarter of the fallen have individual graves.

Initially, the dead of both sides were buried near the spot where they fell, and the plateau was covered with their graves. Almost all of them were moved after the war to a handful of large cemeteries, such as these two near Chambry, in order to make the graves easier to maintain, and to leave the farmers' fields unobstructed. In the French cemetery note the grave of *Chef de bataillon* Henri d'Urbal, who lies in the front row of the second plot from the left as you look from the entrance. Later in this tour we will visit his previous tomb – where he was buried at the time of the battle – when we reach the village of Barcy (Point 7).

The French were conscious that collecting their dead into bigger cemeteries emphasized the sheer scale of their wartime sacrifices – an aspect that was politically important in supporting their insistence on harsh German reparations. Even so, the French and German cemeteries on this battlefield give an incomplete idea of the human cost, partly as many corpses were cremated to prevent an epidemic, and also as the remains of many French soldiers were returned after the war at their families' request, so they could be reburied locally.

Point 5: Chambry

The village of Chambry lies 2 km south-west of the French military cemetery. Go back over the bridge to the southern side of the railway line, and take the first right on to the D140. After passing the first buildings on the outskirts of Chambry, stop at the local civilian cemetery on your right.

Since 1914 the cemetery has been extended north-eastwards, but you can clearly see where the new wall begins. An isolated section of the old wall stands in the middle, with a plaque claiming that its loopholes were made by the *zouaves* of the *45e division*. The question of what really happened here is controversial. The French maintained that they ran into serious resistance at Chambry, but the German *Reichsarchiv* was unable to find any evidence to substantiate these claims, despite making an exhaustive search while compiling its official history of the battle. Chambry and its cemetery did not,

Chambry cemetery: remnant of the old, loopholed wall.

in fact, form part of the German position, which lay 1 km further east, along the rim of high ground above the hollow of Varreddes. The *Reichsarchiv* conceded that some isolated German infantry detachments may have become involved in a firefight at Chambry on 6 September, possibly because they penetrated that far during a counter-attack. But thereafter none of their units would have been so far forward. Apart from being bombarded by artillery, therefore, the cemetery saw little actual fighting.

You will find the graves of several French soldiers here. In front of the loopholed section of wall in the centre are the tombs of *Caporal* Joseph-Louis Andrieu of the *246e régiment*, and *Capitaine* Fernand Bigoudot of the *1er zouaves*. Close to the entrance gates lies another *zouave* from the *45e division*, *Caporal-fourrier* Henri Allaire, and among the other graves is that of *Lieutenant* André Arrighi of the *Brigade marocaine*, who fell on 6 September.

Point 6: *Monument des Quatre Routes*

From the cemetery follow the D140 through the village of Chambry, and then continue for another 1.25 km until you reach the monument at the intersection with the D38.

The 'Monument of the Four Roads' was erected on Galliéni's orders for the first anniversary of the battle, and honours those men of the

The second anniversary of the battle: the Bishop of Arras places a flag at the **Monument des Quatre Routes**.

The monument today.

Armée de Paris who fell in the Battle of the Ourcq. (The *Armée de Paris* – or sometimes its plural form, *Armées de Paris* – was the overall term for the forces under Galliéni, the military governor of the capital, and included both the garrison and the more mobile *6e armée*.) Inscribed on the rear of the monument are a couple of lines from Victor Hugo's poem, *Les chants du crepuscule*, which he wrote in 1831:

'Glory to our everlasting France. Glory to those who have died for her.' The views from this point made it an obvious location for the monument. To the south you can see the tower of Meaux cathedral 3.5 km away, and, beyond it, the heights on the far side of the Marne. To the west-south-west lies Penchard at the base of its wooded hill, at a distance of just 1.5 km.

Point 7: Barcy

At the crossroads in front of the monument, turn right on to the D38 (signposted for Acy-en-Multien), and head northwards away from Meaux. After 3 km the road veers to the north-east, and you will see the village of Barcy 400 metres to the left. To enter the village, turn left at the crossroads with the D97, and pause near the church.

The French occupied Barcy on 6 September, and then launched a series of attacks from its vicinity. They headed for the German positions 2 km further east, but were bloodily repulsed as they tried to cross the viciously exposed plateau. You will find the graves of some of the fallen in the local cemetery. Drive 300 metres down the

Barcy after the battle.

Inside Barcy church after the battle.

rue Chatel from the church green, and you will see the cemetery on your left when you reach the village exit. There is space for parking in front. Inside, near the entrance, is the initial tomb of *Chef de bataillon* Henri d'Urbal of the *2e zouaves*, who was killed during one of the attacks made by his regiment on 7 September. He was buried in this cemetery, in a crater made by a shell, but after the war was transferred to the French military cemetery near Chambry (Point 4).

By the end of the battle Barcy had been devastated by German artillery fire. The intensity of the bombardment is clear from the war diary of one of the *45e division*'s brigades. 'We counted between two and three shots a minute falling regularly on Barcy and its surroundings', reads the entry for 8 September, 'with barely a short lull around the middle of the day – in short, a minimum of a thousand shells on an area of around 10 hectares.' Surprisingly few men were lost – this was partly as hardly anyone was in the village itself, except the brigade staff, and some hundreds of wounded men in a farm awaiting evacuation – but most of the houses were damaged. The church itself was wrecked, and was finally repaired in 1922.

The final sight at Barcy – the *Monument Notre-Dame de la Marne* – lies just outside the village to the east. To reach it, return along the

Barcy: the Monument Notre-Dame de la Marne.

D97 (the route by which you entered the village), cross the D38, and continue another 300 metres to the stone obelisk on the right of the road. Standing on a shallow mound, the monument commands a magnificent view of the battlefield to the north. It was while attacking across the open fields around this spot that the French lost so heavily. On the front of the obelisk is a statue of the Virgin Mary holding Jesus as a child.

Mourning a fallen French soldier. Barcy is in the background.

The monument was the inspiration of the Bishop of Meaux, *Monseigneur* Marbeau. He had remained in his city in September 1914, and one evening, during the tense days while the battle was still raging, he announced to his congregation that if Meaux was saved, he vowed to celebrate the Feast of the Immaculate Conception of the Holy Virgin in the cathedral every year. He also decided to erect a commemorative monument near Barcy. It would be both religious and patriotic in nature, and would thus symbolize the *Union sacrée*, France's laying-aside of its deep social divisions in order to unite against a foreign enemy. It would be an expression of gratitude to God and the fallen soldiers, for preserving Meaux from the Germans. Marbeau's initial idea was a chapel, with the names of the dead inscribed on the walls. In the event, the monument that was erected was the one you see today. More than 4,000 people attended the inauguration in June 1924, but, sadly, Marbeau had died three years earlier, aged 76.

Under the statue are inscribed the words: *Tu n'iras pas plus loin.* The phrase is explained in Marbeau's account of the events at Meaux, published in 1915, in which he wrote that the bodies of the fallen French soldiers 'made an insurmountable rampart that marked the highpoint of the tide of invaders, to whom they said: *You'll go no further.*' This location near Barcy was chosen for the monument, partly as it saw some of the bloodiest fighting, and as many of the French dead were buried at this spot (they are now in the military cemetery of Chambry), but partly, too, because the staff of a German general halted here on the afternoon of 4 September, immediately before the battle, which struck Marbeau as symbolic of the turning of the tide. To the right of the obelisk is a more recent memorial, dedicated to all the combatants of the Battle of the Marne.

Point 8: Etrépilly
Return to the crossroads outside Barcy, and turn right on to the D38. Drive along it for 2 km to the north-east, until you reach another crossroads, and then turn off to the right on to the D401. Follow it eastwards for 3 km into Etrépilly, and stop in the little car park outside the church in the centre of the village, so you can follow the action here on foot.

Etrépilly was heavily contested, since it guarded the point where the Thérouanne valley cut through the German position. It was after dark on the evening of 7 September that the most dramatic clash suddenly flared up. Etrépilly had been occupied earlier that day by a German brigade consisting of *Reserve-Infanterie-Regiments Nr 32* and *82*. The battle died down at dusk, but towards 8.00 pm the night sky was suddenly lit up as the French artillery opened fire on the village. Half an hour later the noise of fighting broke out at the western entrance. Covered by darkness and the shellfire, the *2e zouaves* (from the *45e division*) had advanced from near the crossroads of the D38 and D401, and now burst over the Thérouanne bridge and down the long curve of the village street. In front poured a tide of fleeing German troops, who found themselves channelled along the street by its houses and walls. At last, a side-street branched off to the left, some 400 metres from the village entrance, and led up the slopes, out on to the plateau. Some of the German soldiers took this route, followed by the bulk of the *zouaves*.

The sudden irruption of the *2e zouaves* was part of a more general French attack. On the high ground north-west of Etrépilly, the *350e régiment* (part of the *56e division de réserve*) had captured two machine-guns and driven back the German units opposed to them. The fight reached its climax around the cemetery of Etrépilly, 400 metres north of the village centre. This area served as a rallying point for the Germans. As the *zouaves* emerged on to the plateau, some burning haystacks enabled them to see German units a mere 200 metres away. In the fight that ensued, the commander of the *2e zouaves, Lieutenant-colonel* Victor-Emile Dubujadoux, fell mortally wounded at the foot of the cemetery wall. Fresh German troops intervened, and the *zouaves* were forced back, eventually losing Etrépilly altogether. Towards 10.00 pm the action finally petered out.

To reach the cemetery from the church, walk back along the village street for 150 metres, and then turn right up the D146 (signposted for Vincy-Manœuvre). Inside the cemetery is a marble plaque honouring the dead of the *Armée de Paris*, and immediately to the left is the grave of one of those men, Henri Champain of the *354e régiment* (part of the *56e division*). A handful of other French soldiers, from a variety of units, are buried here, but it is the *2e zouaves* who have the strongest link to Etrépilly, not least as they lost around half their strength on 7 September. On the outside of the cemetery a plaque marks the spot where Dubujadoux fell. 'Alas!' wrote his brigade commander, 'he deserved so much to lead this fine regiment that was so worthy of him. He's a great loss.'

Beyond the cemetery, on the western side of the road and 100 metres further north, is a monument dedicated to the slain soldiers of the *Armée de Paris*. Inaugurated on the first anniversary of the battle, it bears the same lines from Victor Hugo's poem as appear on the *Monument des Quatre Routes* (Point 6). To the rear are buried over 500 French soldiers, most of them in two mass graves. You will find Dubujadoux's grave on the right of the entrance path, at the near end of the first row.

Etrépilly: the plaque on the cemetery wall to Dubujadoux.

The monument at Etrépilly.

Point 9: Champfleury farm

Return westwards along the D401 to the crossroads with the D38, and then head north. Where the road bends to the left, 100 metres after crossing the Thérouanne, turn right up a narrow but tarmacked road to Champfleury. (The turning is not signposted.)

Champfleury stood 2 km west of the German position. On the afternoon of 6 September the advanced posts of the French *56e division* advanced from the west and occupied the farm. But in the days that followed, the plateau outside came under such a hurricane of German shellfire that even individuals were unable to cross it, let alone entire units. The French had to dig in, and for the rest of the battle Champfleury became a bastion anchoring their front line.

The farm was important not simply because it was so solidly built, or because its buildings were arranged around a courtyard to form a readily defensible perimeter, but because of its dominating position. Perched on the very edge of the high ground, it overlooks both the Thérouanne valley to the south and another imposing valley to the west. The view from the farm stretches away to the *Buttes de la Goële*, 8 km to the south-west.

Point 10: Puisieux

Continue another 1.5 km north-eastwards to Puisieux. As you enter the village, follow the road (the *Grande rue*) round, past the church, and stop at the crossroads in the village centre. Note the local war memorial, which honours not just the *commune*'s own dead but all the French soldiers who fought in the Battle of the Ourcq.

It was in the fields just outside Puisieux that a French artillery officer took a decision that helped propel him in little more than two years to high command. He was *Colonel* Robert Nivelle, the commander of the *5e régiment d'artillerie de campagne*. He had already distinguished himself during the August battles, and now did so again in the evening of 6 September. When part of the *63e division de réserve* broke and fled whilst attacking towards the village of Vincy, it was Nivelle who averted disaster. His 75mm batteries were deployed on the high ground 2 km west and north-west of the low-lying Puisieux. Rather than fall back, he took half of his regiment forward at a gallop, down the slopes and into the valley. Passing through the retreating infantrymen, he had his guns unlimber actually in the midst of the French skirmish line, from where they opened a rapid fire. It was a bold move, and enabled the infantry to rally. Confident and charismatic, Nivelle rose to replace Joffre as commander-in-chief in December 1916, only to be sacked the following May after failing to live up to expectations.

The incident at Puisieux has become famous, but was not unique. Time and again during the battle, French gunners intervened to check attacks, thus offsetting the superior tactical training of the German infantry. The 75mm gun was one of the key reasons for the victory of the Marne. It was light, quick-moving and accurate, and could fire at least fifteen rounds a minute. A four-gun battery could plaster a target area with a *rafale*, or 'squall', that proved deadly to troops if

Nivelle: a photograph taken a couple of years after the Marne.

they were caught out in the open. Unfortunately, the French faith in the 75mm was so absolute that that they had hardly any heavy artillery, and hence found it difficult to counter the heavy howitzers fielded by the Germans. It was a deficiency that helps explain the occasional brittleness of their infantry at the Battle of the Ourcq, and one that would pose even greater problems once the front solidified and the two sides dug deep trenches.

Point 11: Nogeon farm

Head north out of Puisieux along the D38 (it becomes the D51 during the drive). After 3 km you arrive at the farm of Nogeon – it stands on the western side of the road junction where the D51 joins the D18. The farm is a vast complex, built around a courtyard, and occupies the high ground dominating the Gergogne valley further north. Secured by the French on 6 September, it was devastated by German artillery fire in the days that followed.

It was during the fighting near Nogeon that the Germans lost a flag. In the evening of 7 September two battalions of *Füsilier-Regiment Nr 36* attacked towards the farm from the south-east, but were foiled by a hail of fire, and had to fall back and rally near Vincy, which you can see on the eastern horizon. The 1st Battalion lost its flag during this attack, but in the confusion and the gathering darkness did not even notice its absence until later. When the battalion reassembled after the repulse of the attack, its commander noticed the flag was missing, but was told by his men that a wounded subaltern

After the battle: the courtyard of Nogeon farm.

had taken it to the rear. Only the next day did it emerge that the subaltern had instead brought back the flag of the 3rd Battalion.

According to the official French version of events, the flag was captured in a hand-to-hand fight by a soldier called Guillemard of the *298e régiment*, who was rewarded with the *Médaille militaire*. Galliéni personally pinned the medal to Guillemard's chest and then, noticing that he was on the verge of tears, made him laugh by whispering in his ear: 'Come on, embrace me, and imagine that I'm a pretty girl!'

It made a fine propaganda story, yet the medal may well have gone to the wrong man. According to the *60e régiment*, the flag was actually captured by one of its officers before being carried away in the tumult by men of the *298e*.

Point 12: Acy-en-Multien

From Nogeon, drive north-eastwards along the D18 to Acy. (You can see the tall steeple of its church amid the woods of the Gergogne valley, 2.5 km directly down the road.) On reaching Acy, turn left

Acy. The French attacked towards the camera.

on to the D332 (signposted for Betz), and drive through the village to the church.

Acy repeatedly changed hands, for the Germans had their main position on top of the plateau to the north-east, leaving the village directly between the two sides. To see this sector of the battlefield from the German perspective, make a side-trip to Etavigny, 2.5 km to the north-east along the D18. Standing on high ground, Etavigny was one of the key points of the German position, and became a particular target for French artillery fire, partly because its church tower was an obvious observation point. By the end of the battle the church was in ruins, and the village partly burned down. In contrast, the church in the valley at Acy escaped serious damage, for it was too low-lying to be of much use for observation.

Return to Acy and go to the northern exit of the village, to the point where the D19 divides from the D332. Pause here to visit the local cemetery, with its plot of soldiers' graves – mostly men killed in this sector during the battle. Then leave Acy along the D332, which passes to the right of the cemetery, in the direction of Betz. Amid the trees on the right-hand side of the road is a *château*, whose park wall runs alongside the road. The Germans prepared this wall for defence, and were able to check several French assaults in front of it with a hail of fire.

Point 13: *Bois de Montrolle*
Three-quarters of the way to Betz, the road passes through the *Bois de Montrolle*. As you emerge from the far side, you will see a large, stone monument 400 metres away, amid a cluster of trees on the left. Park at the roadside some 100 metres short of the monument, where you will find a track forming a lay-by.

The monument marks the site of a mass grave, and is dedicated to the men of the *Armée de Paris* who died on the battlefields of the Ourcq. Other fallen French soldiers are buried individually around the memorial, although many of them died later in the war.

From the rear of the monument the view stretches away to the west, across the plain to Villers-St-Genest and Fresnoy. It was across these open fields that the French *61e division de réserve* attacked east-wards on the afternoon of 7 September, only to be repelled before

The monument near the **Bois de Montrolle.**

they could reach the point where you are standing. Further south, some units penetrated into the *Bois de Montrolle*, before being thrown out by a German counter-attack. Next day, the French tried again, only to be repulsed once more.

Romsey Library 1
RENEW ONLINE at www.hants.gov.uk/library or
phone 0300 555 1387

LOVE YOUR LIBRARY

. . . .
. . . .

Everyone in Hampshire deserves access to high-
quality library services. Help shape them for the
future. www.hants.gov.uk/library-consultation
. . . .
. . . .

Customer ID: *******1139

Items borrowed today

Title: The Battle of Marne 1914
ID: C015632902
Due: 22 February 2020

Total items: 1
Account balance: £0.00
25/01/2020 14:37
Items borrowed: 2
Overdue items: 0
Reservations: 1
Reservations for collection: 0

Items that you already have on loan

Title: Rogue male
ID: C014714867
Due: 10 February 2020

Thank you for using the Library.

Optional visit

We have come almost to the northern edge of the battlefield. To the north lies the village of Betz; beyond it, the open plateau starts to give way to forests that cover great swathes of land for the next 40 km, to beyond the Oise river. The tour ends here, but if you wish, drive to the outskirts of Betz and then westwards along the D922 to Nanteuil-le-Haudouin. The 10 km of plain through which you pass witnessed the German offensive on the afternoon of 9 September, which was meant to roll up the northern wing of the *6e armée*. But it was too late. The advance ground to a halt, and events elsewhere forced the *1. Armee* to retreat. When you reach Nanteuil, visit the memorial to the legendary taxis of the Marne (page 200).

Tour 3

JOFFRE'S OFFENSIVE

The Ourcq, which we have visited in our previous two tours, is just one corner of the vast, sprawling Battlefield of the Marne. On Sunday, 6 September Joffre launched his main offensive south of the river. This tour studies the role played in that onslaught by the *3e corps*, a part of the French *5e armée*. The events in this sector were typical of the first day of the offensive, in that although the French failed to secure an immediate breakthrough, they did make modest gains, advancing up to 6 km and bringing the long retreat to an emphatic end.

The action is of special interest in that it illustrates how, barely a month into the war, the French were already developing more effective ways of using air reconnaissance and artillery to support an attack. It is all the more interesting because of the characters of the two divisional commanders who carried out the *3e corps'* attack – Charles Mangin and Philippe Pétain. Both were destined for greatness, yet were starkly different in background and personality. Mangin was an experienced, colonial soldier. At 48 years old, he was fiery and aggressive, and had a face stamped with an air of ruthless determination. When compared with such a pugnacious character, Pétain is often regarded as cautious and pessimistic, but he has been portrayed more favourably by his defenders as a gritty, down-to-earth realist. He sometimes seemed cold and aloof, and yet he had the knack of being able to talk easily with his men, partly as he came from an unprivileged background. He had risen only slowly through the ranks: he was ten years older than Mangin, and had been on the verge of retirement when war broke out. His tardy progression owed much to the fact that he was an outsider, with his own individualistic views. He had shone while teaching infantry tactics at the *Ecole de guerre*, or Staff College, but had never been under fire before 1914.

Mangin.

Pétain.

WHAT HAPPENED

The *3e corps* stood near the centre of the *5e armée*, with the *18e corps* on its left, and the *1er corps* on the right. Corps were recruited regionally, and the *3e* came from Normandy and Paris. Following the demoralizing disasters of August, it had been revitalized by Joffre's drastic purge of the senior ranks of the French army. The new appointees included Emile-Victor Hache, the little, white-haired general now in charge of the corps, and two divisional commanders, Mangin and Pétain. The *5e armée* also had a new commander – the ebullient, dynamic Louis Franchet d'Espèrey, a man fizzing with energy and optimism.

Admittedly, not everyone was convinced by Franchet d'Espèrey's boundless confidence. Hache, for example, doubted if his *3e corps* would be fit for battle for another three days. In fact, the morning of the 6th brought a pleasant surprise. As Hache drove alongside an advancing infantry column, he was amazed to see how completely the switch to the offensive had transformed the mood of the men. 'The clear, sunny morning promised a fine day', noted his artillery commander, Jean-Gabriel Rouquerol. 'We could easily have mistaken this for some Autumn manoeuvres, and yet as we acknowledged the salutes of the officers and the glances of the men, we considered the fate to which these brave lads were cheerfully marching.'

The ground over which the *3e corps* had to attack was the rolling Brie plateau, with its numerous villages, streams and woods. The main body started from the valley of the Aubetin river, but outposts had spent the night further forward, level with St-Bon and Villouette. The two divisions of the corps attacked side-by-side, but in the afternoon began to draw slightly apart, since each of them had to support a neighbouring corps on its outer flank. In the west Pétain's *6e division* was ordered to second an attack by the *18e corps* on the village of Montceaux, whereas in the east Mangin's *5e division* advanced on the village of Courgivaux, whilst supporting the *1er corps* in its offensive against the town of Esternay. This emphasis on liaison with other formations highlighted one of the improvements that had been made in the French army since the start of the war. Commanders increasingly recognized the importance of co-ordination to maximize the power of an offensive, and to make gains that were both general and permanent. They sought to avoid the mistakes made in some earlier battles, where corps had fought separate, disjointed actions.

Other tactical lessons had also been learned. The French defeats in August had resulted, at least in part, from over-hasty assaults, launched with insufficient artillery preparation and in formations that were too dense. The emphasis now lay on methodical and co-ordinated attacks. At the Marne the *3e corps* operated on a narrow front, just 5 or 6 km wide, and each of its divisions, rather than attacking several points simultaneously, focused on one objective at a time, so that it advanced in a series of bounds, from hill to hill.

Once it had occupied the next hill, it prepared the conquered ground for defence, as a solid base for a further advance.

It was a carefully controlled process. Each division was deployed in depth, so as to reduce the exposure of its troops, while making it

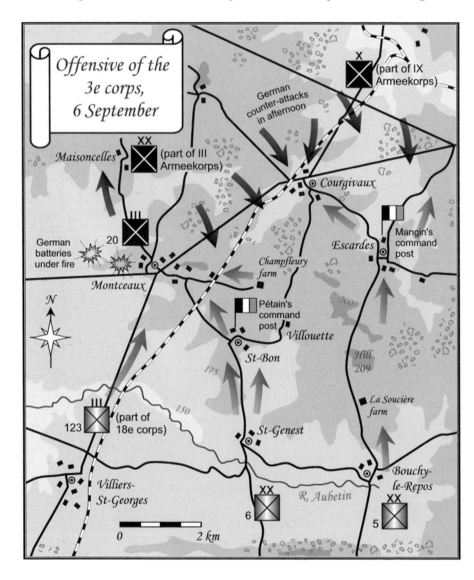

Offensive of the
3e corps,
6 September

Maisoncelles
XX (part of III Armeekorps)

German
counter-attacks
in afternoon

X (part of IX Armeekorps)

Courgivaux

III 20

German
batteries
under fire

Montceaux

Escardes

Mangin's
command
post

Champfleury
farm

N

Pétain's
command
post

Villouette

St-Bon

Hill
209

La Soucière
farm

III 123 (part of 18e corps)

St-Genest

Villiers-
St-Georges

XX 6

R. Aubetin

Bouchy-
le-Repos

XX 5

0   2 km

more resilient in the event of a German counter-attack, and ensuring that it had enough fresh units in hand to maintain the offensive over the course of several days. Only those units actually required to make an assault were out in front, so the others could take advantage of any cover further to the rear. The idea was that a limited number of infantrymen would make the actual attack, but with overwhelming artillery support. 'Artillery conquers, infantry occupies', Pétain explained. Of the twelve battalions in his division, only three were engaged, and even in those three, just some of the companies were pushed forward. For example, the *24e régiment* used a single battalion as its advanced guard and assault force, and that battalion had just two-and-a-half companies, or little more than half its strength, in the first line. The regiment lost between 300 and 350 officers and men, but fewer than 10 per cent of these casualties were incurred by the two supporting battalions. In Pétain's second brigade, which followed in support, the *5e régiment* lost a mere six men.

Vigorous reaction

By chance, the German units attacked by the *3e corps* were from the *III Armeekorps*. This was one of Kluck's corps, and that morning was due to begin a march 15 km back to the north-west, as part of a gradual redeployment of Kluck's *1. Armee* – a precautionary measure that would turn into a complete withdrawal to the Battlefield of the Ourcq once Kluck realized the gravity of the situation there.

The Germans expected a quiet, leisurely day, in the belief that the French would continue their retreat across the Seine. Much of the *III Armeekorps* actually began its planned march to the north-west, and had to be halted, and then recalled, after heavy artillery fire opened and it slowly grew clear that the French had launched a major offensive.

The *III Armeekorps* had left behind two detachments at the twin villages of Courgivaux and Montceaux to cover its march. The one at Courgivaux set off in the wake of the corps, but the detachment at Montceaux was attacked before it had a chance to leave. As the action grew more intense, the French artillery tried to counter the German batteries that were shelling the advancing infantry. The commander of Pétain's divisional artillery was *Colonel* Eugène Estienne, a pioneer of military aviation who would also help create France's tank arm later in the war. In order to locate targets for his guns, Estienne had taken two airplanes with him on campaign, one of which flew a reconnaissance mission on the morning of 6 September. The pilot returned with a sketch showing the positions of the German batteries, which were mostly concentrated on the reverse slopes close behind Montceaux. Copies of the sketch were quickly distributed to the French artillery. Another airplane, belonging to the *5e armée* and placed at the disposal of the *3e corps*, likewise reported on the German locations.

Montceaux caught fire under the intense shelling, sending clouds of smoke drifting through the air. The French bombardment trapped a German divisional commander and his staff inside the village for the entire morning, making it difficult for them to control the action until they finally escaped around noon. By the middle of the afternoon, Montceaux had become untenable, and was abandoned by the detachment holding it, *Infanterie-Regiment Nr 20*. Pétain's infantry had already occupied Champfleury farm, just 2.5 km to the east, and at 5.30 pm they reached Les Châtaigniers (a farm 750 metres from the village centre).

But the situation was less favourable for the French on their right wing, where Mangin now faced a crisis. At first, his advance had

French infantry advance to the attack.

gone well. Soon after 10.00 am his leading units reached the village of Escardes, and in the afternoon they occupied Courgivaux. They encountered barely any resistance, for the German detachment here had already marched off before the battle began, yet their success proved short-lived. Despite being surprised by the offensive, the two German corps in this region – the *III Armeekorps* and the *IX* further east – reacted vigorously, and launched a major counter-attack on either side of Courgivaux. At 5.00 pm they retook the village, and in some places penetrated several hundred metres beyond the lateral road linking Montceaux and Courgivaux (now designated the N4). They were eventually checked not so much by resistance on the ground – some French infantry units quickly collapsed under the impact – as by the sheer intensity of the artillery fire directed on them once they emerged from the cover of woods or hills.

Massive bombardment
It was Mangin who bore the brunt of the German onslaught, but Pétain's foremost units were also counter-attacked, and fell back that evening from Les Châtaigniers and the nearby railway station to less exposed positions at Champfleury and St-Bon. Pétain knew that he had already done enough to ease the advance of the neighbouring *18e corps*, and that he could resume the offensive the next day. 'The sun is going to bed,' he told his staff, 'let us go and do the same.'

The main thrust of the *18e corps* was directed against Montceaux from the south-west, along the *chaussée* from Villiers-St-Georges. The attack was launched late that afternoon, after the German positions had been softened up by the massive French artillery bombardment. More than 200 guns had ended up pounding Montceaux. After night-fall, part of the *123e régiment* finally entered, only to find it empty, except for some Germans who had sheltered in cellars during the shelling, and who were now taken prisoner.

The impact of Joffre's offensive was psychological as much as physical. The fact that his supposedly demoralized armies were able to attack at all came as a shock to the Germans. So, too, did the sheer intensity of the French artillery fire, which was a new and unpleasant experience for the soldiers at the receiving end. *Hauptmann* Hans Schöning was some 4 km west of Montceaux, and noted how the French artillery fire grew ever brisker. 'During the afternoon, it

Montceaux: the church after the battle.

The damage inside Montceaux church.

intensified its fire more and more, and in the end attained a level that could no longer be distinguished from the so-called drumfire of a later period [in the war] – the only difference was that this fire was dispersed as zone fire over a wide extent, instead of being directed at a narrow sector. For the first time in this conflict, we became conscious of being in the age of industrialized warfare.'

Next morning, the German units opposed to the *3e corps* fell back to a less exposed position some 20 km to the rear, and then left the area altogether when summoned to reinforce their embattled comrades on the Battlefield of the Ourcq. Their departure left a dangerous gap between the *1.* and *2. Armeen*, a gap that the *5e armée* would gradually prise open during the next couple of days, in conjunction with the BEF further west.

WHAT TO SEE

This tour follows the advance of Pétain's division to Montceaux, and then examines the parallel events in Mangin's sector, near Courgivaux. The starting point is the town of Villiers-St-Georges. To reach it from Paris, drive eastwards along the N4, in the direction of Esternay and Sézanne. About 3.5 km after passing the village of Courtacon turn right on to the D15, and follow it south-eastwards.

Point 1: Villiers-St-Georges
Villiers-St-Georges lay in the sector of the *18e corps*, on Pétain's western flank. Its church was damaged by German artillery fire, and the tower had to be rebuilt. You will find a French military cemetery at the town's northern exit, beside the roundabout where the D403 crosses the D60. (Car parking is available 100 metres to the south, opposite the civilian cemetery.) Inside, the local war memorial also commemorates the French soldiers killed in the vicinity during the battle, as well as wounded men who died at a field hospital later in the war. 'This historic location', records a barely legible inscription on the base of the monument, 'was the starting point on 6 September 1914 for the French troops who saved the country at the Battle of the Marne.'

We will now drive to the village of St-Genest, 4 km to the east, to see the area from where Pétain began his advance. At the round-about outside the cemetery, take the D60 to the south-east (sign-posted for Louan-Villegruis-Fontaine and Villenauxe-la-Grande). After 700 metres turn left on to the D60a (signposted for Brasseaux and St-Genest). As you approach Brasseaux, note the panoramic

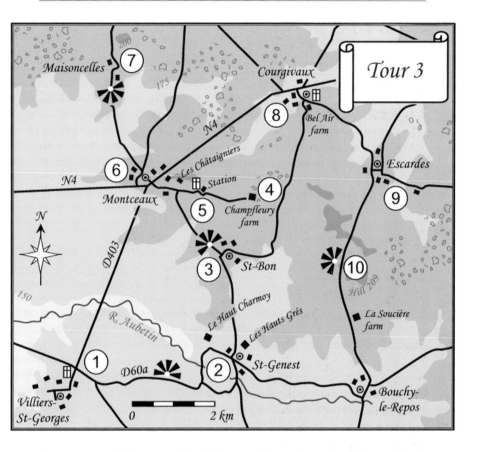

view on your left, extending 5 km northwards to the hilltop village of Montceaux. After the road has wound its way through Brasseaux, it crosses the Aubetin river, bends round to the right at the farm of Le Haut Charmoy, and brings you to St-Genest.

Point 2: St-Genest

On the morning of 6 September Pétain's advanced guard held the farms of Le Haut Charmoy and Le Haut Gré, on the high ground immediately north of the Aubetin river. (The second of these two farms, now called Les Hauts Grés, dominates the northern exit of St-Genest, on the right of the road to St-Bon.) These farms were the departure line for Pétain's offensive. Outposts were further forward, but the bulk of his division was more to the rear – his own headquarters were at Louan, 4 km to the south. As the leading units advanced in bounds, they drew the rest of the division forward in their wake.

Point 3: St-Bon

At the western entrance to St-Genest, take the road signposted for St-Bon, 2.5 km to the north. This marks the next bound forward in Pétain's advance, and it was on the slopes near St-Bon that one of the most legendary incidents of his career occurred. When he saw his infantry hesitate in the face of the German shellfire, he walked forward with his escort to set a personal example of courage. 'He advanced across the fields towards St-Bon', explained a liaison officer. 'The whole line of artillery, and all the troops in reserve in the low ground, saw this white-haired man as he went forward, calm and determined, to the ridge that was being shelled and that the skirmishers still hesitated to cross. It was a magnificent sight, under a blazing sun and beneath the steel canopy formed by our 75mm shells, whose flight through the air produced a real, ceaseless roar amid the explosions of the heavy shells from the German howitzers.'

At 10.15 am Pétain established his command post at the eastern exit of St-Bon. The courage he showed at this little village became a celebrated part of his life-story, yet actually it was far from unique. (Mangin took his command post as far forward as Escardes, and during the German counter-attack that afternoon joined his skirmish lines to help check the tide of fugitives, while calmly smoking his pipe.) Even so, accounts of Pétain's heroism, and his undoubted success at the Marne, helped accelerate his remarkable rise. In less than a year he was commanding an army, and at the end of the war he was raised to the dignity of *maréchal*, only to become one of the most divisive figures in French history as head of the Vichy regime in 1940–4.

Drive through St-Bon, following the signpost for Montceaux. As you leave the north-western exit of the village, you can clearly see Montceaux church on the hill-top 2 km ahead. The occupation of St-Bon enabled several French batteries to establish themselves on the slopes south of the village, from where they pounded the Germans around Montceaux. The French fire was all the more effective in that it was directed at the German positions from an angle, rather than from directly in front.

Point 4: Champfleury farm

Continue along the D119 until you come to a crossroads at the southeastern tip of Montceaux. The massive farm in front of you is Les Châtaigniers. But our first stop lies 1.7 km further east, so turn right on to the no-through road (signposted for Champfleury and the *Cimitière militaire national*), and continue along it until you come to the farm of Champfleury at the end of the road.

A battalion of Pétain's *28e régiment* reached Champfleury between 12.00 and 1.00 pm, following the French occupation of St-Bon and the neighbouring hamlet of Villouette. Champfleury stands on high ground, and made a convenient base for the next stage of Pétain's advance – an attack on Les Châtaigniers. That attack, launched at 4.00 pm, involved three battalions advancing from St-Bon and Champfleury, and we will now follow its progress by retracing our route back to the west.

Point 5: Railway station

At the time of the battle a railway line passed between Champfleury and Les Châtaigniers, heading north-eastwards from Villiers-St-Georges. Its embankment became one of the successive French objectives as they closed in on Montceaux. Although the line was dismantled in 1970, its course remains clear from the line of trees and bushes cutting across the fields. The local station still exists, but is now a private residence – you will find it at the bend in the road 1.2 km west of Champfleury.

The station was the scene of a remarkable coincidence at the end of the action. It was seized that afternoon by a battalion of the French *24e régiment* attacking from the direction of St-Bon. In the evening Pétain's most advanced units pulled back in the face of counter-attacks, and a detachment of the German *Infanterie-Regiment Nr 24* reached the station. The Germans could hear French voices within the building, so they burst in from two sides, smashing the windows as they did so. Inside, they found a dead *lieutenant*, and a dozen wounded soldiers, but they noticed that the Frenchmen's collars

The former railway station at Montceaux.

bore the number 24. One of the Germans bent down, and unfastened his shoulder strap to show that his regiment, too, was the 24th. 'Good evening, comrades!' he exclaimed in French. 'Twenty-four!'

'Good evening, good evening! Good comrades!' the French replied in delight, and probably in some relief. The Germans fetched water and wine from the cellar. The *Feldwebel*, or sergeant-major, awaited his turn, and then filled his mess kit right to the brim with wine – more than 2 litres in all. He began drinking it, and continued steadily even when the outposts called that a body of French troops was coming. 'They're nearly here!' came the warning. At last the *Feldwebel* finished his wine, and then he went to the corner of the station. Up the moonlit road marched more than twenty French soldiers. The *Feldwebel* challenged them in their own language, and, on receiving a reply, told them to pass. Suspecting nothing, they

Montceaux's war memorial, in the local military cemetery.

marched on, only to be taken by surprise as the Germans leaped among them, screaming that they were prisoners.

Just 100 metres north-west of the station, on the right-hand side of the road, is a French military cemetery. Only some of the men buried here fell on 6 September; many of the others died from wounds received in 1918.

Point 6: Montceaux

Drive further west, past Les Châtaigniers, and directly onwards into Montceaux along the D119. When you come to the crossroads with the N4, continue straight ahead along the D119 (signposted for St-Martin-du-Boschet) and go up the hill to the church. On your left you pass the *mairie*, where a plaque records that three-quarters of Montceaux's houses were destroyed or badly damaged.

The sheer weight of artillery fire directed at Montceaux made it a hellish place for the German defenders. So many shell splinters and chipped pieces of wall were flying around that the streets seemed impassable. The village was held by *Infanterie-Regiment Nr 20*, one of whose officers, *Oberleutnant* Heinrich Heubner, has left a remarkable account of his experiences. He remembered it as one of the most fearsome days of his life. As the French artillery fire steadily intensified, he felt exposed and defenceless. He was sheltering inside a shed, behind the *Ferme de Villebion* – the large farm you can see at the village exit, 130 metres north-west of the church. He listened tensely to the shells bursting all around, fearing that at any moment one would fly over the farm buildings and into his shed. After several hours of this, he was in such a state of nervous exhaustion that he actually managed to sleep for a quarter of an hour, despite the noise.

Towards 4.00 pm the artillery fire reached a climax as the French infantry drew closer to Montceaux. Orders came to abandon the now-untenable village. 'Then began the most dreadful moments of this terrifying day', Heubner recalled. 'We had to emerge from cover, and cross the low-lying ground to the rear, passing though the endless hail of enemy shells. There could be no question of setting off in assembled units under such heavy fire. Instead, every man had to use his initiative to try to get through to the next village [Maisoncelles], which had been given as the rallying point.' Heubner set off with his group of men, but had hardly emerged from the cover of the houses than he found himself in the fiercest fire:

> The enemy's missiles exploded all around me, to the right, the left, in front and behind, and on one occasion so close that I was entirely covered with earth. All I could do, once I heard a shot whistling nearby, was immediately throw

myself down in the turnip field, and then, once it had exploded, leap to my feet and dash forward 10 metres, in order to hurl myself to the ground once more. We raced for our lives like this for a full quarter of an hour. But Heaven preserved us: we came unharmed out of the belt of fire, and, gasping for breath from our excitement and exertion, were able to make our way at a walk to the rallying point.

Point 7: Maisoncelles
Follow Heubner by driving northwards along the D119 from Montceaux (signposted for St-Martin-du-Boschet). When you reach the entrance of Maisoncelles at the top of the hill, look back the way you have come. In the afternoon of the 6th the whole area in front of you was a scene of bedlam. On the horizon, 2 km to the south, Montceaux was shrouded in smoke and flames, and the intervening ground was being pummelled by artillery shells, as if by a hailstorm. Everywhere could be seen explosions, and black columns of smoke.

The bulk of Heubner's regiment gradually reassembled near Maisoncelles, and he spent the evening watching the German artillery pounding Montceaux now that it had been abandoned to the French. 'From time to time, a mighty, dull bang sounded behind us', he wrote. 'Then our heavy artillery shells whistled high over our heads, to shower their hail of iron on the unfortunate Montceaux. Most of the hilltop village now burned furiously, flames rose into the sky from the church, farm, and other houses, and thick clouds of smoke settled over the plain, darkening even the pale light of the moon.'

Point 8: Courgivaux
It is now time to see Mangin's sector, and the scene of the German counter-attack at the village of Courgivaux, 5 km to the east. From Maisoncelles, drive back to Montceaux, and then turn left, on to the N4. When you reach Courgivaux, turn right on to the D648 just after the car park and information area (the turning is signposted for Escardes), and go through the centre of the village, uphill past the church.

Mangin's leading elements occupied Courgivaux early in the afternoon without a fight. But that evening a couple of battalions of the

74e régiment, entrusted with holding the village, lost it to the German counter-attack. Many of the houses were wrecked, although the church suffered barely any harm.

Continue out of Courgivaux along the D648 (signposted for Escardes), and after 200 metres stop outside the cemetery on the left of the road. The original local cemetery (the military part has simply been added in front) was one of the key strongholds at Courgivaux, as was the large farm of Bel Air, the modern outbuildings of which are visible 200 metres to the south-west. Both these points stand on high ground above the village: together, they blocked its southern entrance, and were badly damaged by artillery fire.

A plaque on the cemetery wall states that Courgivaux was on the point of being recaptured by the Germans when *Capitaine* Vaillant of the *74e régiment* had some machine-guns placed in the attics of the houses. 'Courgivaux was saved', claims the plaque, 'but *Capitaine* Vaillant, superb under fire, fell gloriously wounded.' In fact, the inscription is misleading, for Courgivaux did fall to the Germans. A company of engineers, which Mangin had sent to the village to put it in a state of defence, tried to hold the cemetery, but was obliged to fall back since the Germans were pursuing the French fugitives so closely that it was impossible to fire at the one without hitting the other.

In the middle of the military cemetery is Courgivaux's war memorial – a column, surmounted by a Gallic cock. It also commemorates the French soldiers who fought in this sector in 1914, over 190 of whom

lie in a mass grave. They include Louis Barrière, whose fate we shall discover in the optional visit at the end of this tour. Among those buried individually is *Capitaine* Marie-Alphonse Haas, a company commander in the *129e régiment* (Grave number 20). On the morning of 7 September his *colonel* found him where he had spent the night, sitting at the edge of a trench outside Courgivaux,

Capitaine *Haas.*

Capitaine *Haas' grave at Courgivaux military cemetery.*

with his head leaning on his shoulder. On calling his name, the *colonel* received no reply, and then found that Haas had been shot through the heart. His face was pale, but not a drop of blood was visible on his uniform and he seemed to be asleep.

Point 9: Escardes
From the cemetery, continue along the D648 to Escardes, 2.25 km to the south-east. Stop at the *mairie*, which stands on the left of the road as you enter the village, just before you come to the church. Note the two plaques on the front of the building – they commemorate the occupation of the village by the *39e régiment*, and Mangin's repulse of the German counter-attack in the afternoon.

Mangin had climbed the church tower to observe the progress of the action, but when the Germans launched their counter-offensive, he went to the northern edge of Escardes, and watched his foremost units falling back towards him. He later described how:

> I remained with sixty men in a semblance of a trench, at the edge of the village, for we had formal orders not to withdraw another inch, and if I yielded, the other divisions would have had to conform to remain in line with me. The German infantry manoeuvred as if on the drill ground, the skirmishers rapidly reaching each piece of cover, while the supports and reserves followed the movement, and exploited the undulations of the ground. At first, we mistook them for French detachments, and I needed my good pair of binoculars before I dared give the order to open fire. But their artillery lost contact with their infantry, and did not give it support. Our guns, in contrast, deployed as normal, opened a terrible fire at a range of 600 metres, and thereby checked the enemy skirmishers. At the same moment, two of our machine-guns went into action, and did marvels.

The tripods of these machine-guns had been lost during the fighting in August, so they needed a makeshift footing. The *lieutenant* in command of them therefore pierced loopholes in the northern end of the *mairie* – holes that are still visible today. At the time of the battle the *mairie* also housed a school. An irate civilian, who turned out to be the acting schoolmaster, accosted Mangin. 'It's all very well to make holes in the walls', he complained. 'But who will pay for the damage?'

The din spared Mangin from having to argue the matter, for the machine-guns began to rattle and the French artillery accelerated its fire against the oncoming German counter-attack. He saw the German skirmisher line vanish: 'The supports, coming under fire in their turn, were pinned down with enormous losses, and ended up fleeing into the neighbouring wood, which soon became a hellish place. My staff officers rallied our detachments, which turned around and pursued the enemy.' Mangin's men continued to bring in groups of prisoners throughout the evening, and he interrogated the captured officers in the school.

Escardes: the loopholed gable of the mairie.

Point 10: Hill 209

At Escardes turn off the D648 at the point where it bends round the church, and take the road signposted for Bouchy-St-Genest. It soon leads past Escardes' cemetery, where the local war memorial pays tribute to the French troops who fought here. After another 1.75 km you pass a red-and-white communications mast. Continue across a dip in the ground to the next rise, and stop when you reach the crest and see a track joining the road diagonally from the right. Just 400 metres east of your location is Hill 209, the highest point on the battlefield, although its altitude is given on some modern maps as 207 metres. Note the excellent views to Montceaux. It was in this area that part of the artillery of the *3e corps* was deployed. The guns themselves tended to be hidden behind a hill, while observers on the high ground checked the accuracy of the fire. From this central position the batteries could support both divisions of the corps, to

French 75mm artillery in action.

the north and the north-west. (Other batteries were pushed further forward, and were more directly at the disposal of the divisional commanders.) Pétain was in no doubt about the importance of this fire. 'The field artillery was the main reason for the victory of the Marne', he claimed.

Hill 209 offered such good views that Mangin had initially established his command post here in the middle of the morning, before moving further north to Escardes as his division gained ground. Then, at 4.00 pm, the corps commander, Hache, arrived from the rear, and observed the progress of the action through binoculars. Towards 5.00 pm no less a figure than the army commander appeared. Franchet d'Espèrey was visiting his subordinates and seeing the situation for himself. 'So,' he asked. 'Is it going well?' When Hache replied that the situation was still unclear, Franchet d'Espèrey brushed such doubts aside. 'Of course it's going well', he reassured him. 'It's going well, too, with the other corps. Goodbye!'

In fact, the situation soon worsened, for Courgivaux fell to the German counter-attack, and for a while Hache feared that the onslaught might split his corps and separate its two divisions. To help stabilize the situation, an infantry brigade was brought forward from reserve. As it moved over Hill 209, shrapnel rounds exploded overhead. They burst too high to be of much effect, but the men seemed intimidated. 'We went into their midst to encourage them', wrote Hache's artillery commander, 'and make them raise their heads, and the brigade disappeared towards Escardes.' It was yet another example of generals setting a personal example of bravery – just as Pétain had famously done that morning at St-Bon.

Optional visit

This marks the end of the tour, but on the way back to your base you may wish to pass the farm of La Soucière. It stands on the eastern side of the road, 1.5 km south of Hill 209, and was used as a French dressing station. One of the men who helped succour the wounded in the *3e corps'* sector of the battlefield was Maurice Maréchal. He later won international fame as a violoncellist, but at the time of the Marne was a 21-year-old medical orderly serving with the *274e régiment*. In his journal for 7 September he described his elation at the news that the Germans had been driven back. 'Victory, victory!' he sang as he advanced, only to be sobered by the grim sight of fallen French infantrymen strewn all around him. He remembered one of the casualties in particular – a soldier of the *74e régiment*, Louis Barrière, who was the same age as himself. Barrière was dying from a head wound, groaning continuously as he did so, and was later buried at Courgivaux military cemetery (Point 8). 'Oh, the wretched people who sought this war!' Maréchal wrote. 'There are no torments appropriate for you!'

Tour 4

THE BRITISH ADVANCE

The British Expeditionary Force (BEF) constituted less than 9 per cent of the Allied forces at the Marne. Yet it played a disproportionately important role, partly because of its independence (it was not under Joffre's direct command), and partly because of the gap that gradually opened in its path between the two westernmost German armies. Controversy has raged ever since about the BEF's slowness to exploit this gap – it advanced just 11–18 km a day – and about whether this deprived the Allies of a decisive victory.

It is true that the BEF had serious deficiencies in command and staff work, and that its commander, Field Marshal Sir John French, was distinctly cautious about exposing his flanks. But we must recognize that the gap was not completely open: it was covered by two German cavalry corps, which included artillery, machine-guns and light infantry battalions. Despite being outnumbered, these forces were sufficient to impose a succession of delays by exploiting the nature of the terrain.

In front of the BEF lay no fewer than three deep river valleys – the Grand Morin, the Petit Morin and the Marne – and the farmland in between was studded with villages, woods and hedges. Nor did the road network provide much help: the great *chaussées* that radiated out from Paris tended to run *across* the direction of the BEF's advance, rather than along it. Narrow by-roads, winding their way through the countryside and over minor bridges, were hardly designed for the swift passage of an army of over 80,000 men with all its guns and vehicles.

Morale among the British troops rose as their retreat gave way on 6 September to an advance. Minor clashes occurred, but not until the 8th did the BEF run into a general engagement, when the Germans fought a delaying action on the Petit Morin. In this tour we examine that action, focusing in detail on a sector towards the eastern end of the line, where the 2nd Division forced a crossing at La Trétoire.

WHAT HAPPENED

The sun rose on the 8th at 5.15 am. Frederic Coleman, an American serving with the BEF as a volunteer motorcar driver, was filled with excitement. 'We were treated to a wonderful surprise', he wrote:

> The sky along the eastern horizon showed salmon pink and palest blue. The fields by the roadside were full of cavalry units and batteries of guns. Regiments advancing over the meadows in line of squadrons, an imposing array; batteries, belated, galloping into position with an inspiring rattle and bang over any and all obstructions; motor-cycles dodging and panting past less swift users of the road; and even the push-bicyclists putting every ounce of energy into their

Off to war: the 2/Grenadier Guards marching past King George V outside Buckingham Palace on Sunday, 9 August 1914.

pedalling – it was good to be alive that morning as the salmon in the east changed to pale gold and the blue to turquoise.

But trouble lay ahead. Some 10 km to the north the German *I Kavallerie-Korps* was preparing to defend the Petit Morin valley. Its two overstretched divisions covered a front of more than 15 km, from La Ferté-sous-Jouarre in the north-west to the village of Villeneuve in the south-east. Too weak to check the BEF completely, they nonetheless could win vital time. Since their cavalry regiments lacked the firepower and entrenching tools for prolonged actions, the burden of the defence fell on the attached artillery and machine-gun units, and on the two light infantry battalions, the *Garde-Jäger* and *Garde-Schützen*.

The Petit Morin valley was some 80–100 metres deep, but its apparent strength hid serious disadvantages. Its steep sides were largely covered with woods, which meant that the Germans had to place some troops actually on the valley floor, as they were unable from above to observe the river amid the trees, let alone keep it under fire. But once the units inside the valley became seriously engaged, they would find it difficult to break contact and retreat before they were cut off. Nor, it turned out, could their retreat be supported effectively by the cavalry brigades, which were deployed on the top of the exposed plateau: the cavalry would come under such intense artillery fire as to preclude any idea of charging the British units that emerged from the valley. 'The shrapnel fire came as if out of a watering-can', complained one German officer.

The 2nd Division
The three corps of the BEF advanced on a front of 25 km. III Corps in the west headed for the town of La Ferté-sous-Jouarre, where the Petit Morin flowed into the Marne, while II Corps was in the centre. The eastern wing was formed by I Corps, whose two divisions marched side by side – 1st Division on the right and 2nd Division on the left. The advanced guard of the 2nd Division consisted of 4 (Guards) Brigade, covered by an hussar squadron and a cyclist company, and strengthened by an artillery brigade and a company of engineers. Behind came the main body of the division, including

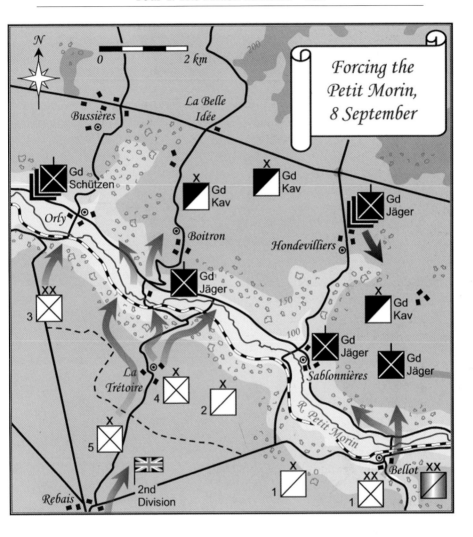

the remaining two infantry brigades (5th and 6th). Since just one infantry brigade occupied as much as 3.5 km of road, the main body as a whole took more than three hours to pass its starting point.

Out in front cavalry patrols brushed back some German reconnaissances, but were checked once they reached the edge of the plateau where it gave way to the Petit Morin valley. Towards 7.30 am the head of the advanced guard appeared, but at the village of

La Trétoire it suddenly came under shrapnel fire from a German battery posted on the opposite heights near Boitron.

From La Trétoire, the road zigzags down the slope to the hamlet of Coton on the valley floor, and then crosses the Petit Morin by a bridge at a locality called Le Gravier. Responsibility for defending this stretch of river rested with the *Garde-Kavallerie-Division*, which was holding a sector 8 km long, from Orly exclusive to Villeneuve inclusive. The burden of the defence of Le Gravier bridge fell to the 4th Company of the *Garde-Jäger-Bataillon*, and to the six machine-guns of the *Garde-Maschinengewehr-Abteilung 1*.

In order to crack this position, 4 Brigade gradually fed its four battalions into the fight, one by one. The first to be sent in, the 3/Coldstream, was checked halfway down the wooded slopes when it encountered a clearing at La Pilloterie, 70 metres wide and swept by German machine-gun fire. Part of the 1/Irish Guards was then committed, on the left of the Coldstream. (Among the officers of the Irish Guards was a popular, 22-year-old platoon commander, Lieutenant the Hon. Harold Alexander, a future field marshal.)

Yet the Guards were unable to break the deadlock, so both battalions were pulled back to give the artillery a chance to soften up the defence. Thus far, the 2nd Division had just three 18-pounder batteries in action, or a total of eighteen guns. They fired shrapnel, but this tended to be effective only against units caught out in the open, such as the German battery near Boitron, and the supporting cavalry brigades. The problem was that the Guards had been checked primarily by machine-gun fire. The 18-pounders had too flat a trajectory to reach the German machine-guns deep inside the valley, whose location could not, in any case, be pinpointed amid the woods. To knock them out, the British needed their 4.5-inch howitzers, whose high-angle, plunging fire would enable them to search the woods with high-explosive shells. At this stage in the war the Royal Artillery was organized into separate gun and howitzer brigades, and the single howitzer brigade had to come up from near the tail of the 2nd Division's column. In the meantime, little more could be done than deploy some of the 18-pounders right on the edge of the valley, while manhandling one of them down the slope to the clearing. Only in 1915 did the British army begin to adopt the

The Coldstream Guards in action.

Stokes mortar, a portable weapon ideal for giving the infantry prompt, short-range fire support in terrain such as this.

After the artillery had done its best, the 3/Coldstream and 1/Irish Guards resumed the attack, and were joined by a couple of companies of the 2/Grenadiers. No fewer than ten Guards companies had now been fed into the woods – too many for a frontage of less than 750 metres. Command and control grew increasingly difficult as units became confused and broken up amid the woods. Platoon commanders often had to act on their own initiative, but the firing made it difficult for their scattered soldiers to hear shouted orders.

To the commander of the 3/Coldstream, there seemed little chance of forcing a crossing at Le Gravier by a frontal attack. He sent back a message advising that it would be better to try the alternative bridge at La Forge, 1.5 km further east. In response, the acting commander of 4 Brigade, Lieutenant Colonel Geoffrey Feilding, ordered the remainder of the 2/Grenadiers to head there through the trees, bypassing the clearing at La Pilloterie. The final battalion of the brigade, the 2/Coldstream, also moved towards La Forge, but from a point further in the rear.

Feilding at this time was standing on the road halfway down the slope. Towards 11.30 am he thought he saw signs that the Germans were withdrawing, and therefore shouted to the commander of the 2/Grenadiers, Major George ('Ma') Jeffreys, to abandon the advance on La Forge, and attack directly across the clearing. But Jeffreys was able to divert little more than his final platoon, and in dashing through the clearing he found that the Germans were still in position, as became obvious from the hail of fire. He was fortunate to reach the trees on the far side without losing any men.

The *Garde-Jäger* company had, in fact, received orders to retire around this time, but it did so gradually, and under the cover of a rearguard. As a result of Feilding's over-hasty change of mind, the 2/Grenadiers had become split into three separate detachments, and the battalion commander was with the smallest of them. One reason why Feilding mismanaged the action was that he had been in command of 4 Brigade for just three days. Nor did it help that he was being urged on by both his divisional and corps commanders, Major General Charles Munro and Lieutenant General Sir Douglas Haig, which helps explain his agitation. (Haig moved forwards that morning to a crossroads 1 km south of La Trétoire, where he was joined for a time by Sir John French.) The pressure was coming ultimately from Joffre, who was concerned that the *6e armée* might be overwhelmed on the Ourcq unless the BEF advanced more vigorously to threaten the rear of the German *1. Armee*.

Bridges secured

By the end of the morning the 2nd Division had brought up an array of fifty-eight guns around La Trétoire, including its eighteen 4.5-inch howitzers. Another infantry brigade was drawn into the action. For the past couple of hours 5 Brigade had been waiting in support 600 metres south of La Trétoire. One of its four battalions, the 2/Worcestershire, was sent to turn the western flank of the *Garde-Jäger* in the valley. From La Trétoire, it moved to the left along the edge of the plateau, before descending the slopes to reach the river opposite Bécherelle, 750 metres north-west of Le Gravier. Towards 12.00 pm a second battalion, the 2/Highland Light Infantry, was sent

1. French 75mm gun. The three remarkable photographs on this page were originally published in 1915. They were taken by Jules Gervais-Courtellemont, a pioneer in direct colour photography.

2. French *zouaves*.

3. Soldiers of the *Brigade marocaine* (Tour 1).

4. Meaux: a view of the cathedral across the Marne (Tour 2).

5. *Musée de la Grande guerre*, at Meaux (Tour 2).

Monument
américain

6. *La Grande tombe* (Tour 1).

7. French graves at Penchard after the battle
(Tour 1). (*Photo: Gervais-Courtellemont*)

8. French infantryman of 1914.

9. Chambry cemetery after the battle (Tour 2). (*Photo: Gervais-Courtellemont*)

10. The cemetery today, still with the loopholes.

11. Barcy church after the battle (Tour 2). (*Photo: Gervais-Courtellemont*)

12. Barcy church today.

13. Etavigny church in ruins (Tour 2). (*Photo: Gervais-Courtellemont*)

14. German military cemetery at Connantre (Tour 6).

15. The Petit Morin river flowing through the St-Gond marshes (Tour 6). (*Photo: Gervais-Courtellemont*)

16. Soizy-aux-Bois (Tour 7). (*Photo: Gervais-Courtellemont*)

17. Mondement: the northern side of the damaged *château* (Tour 7). (*Photo: Gervais-Courtellemont*)

18. The *Château de Mondement* today, seen from the churchyard (Tour 7).

La victoire passait

19. Mondement: the monument to the victory of the Marne (Tour 7).

20. Joffre.

to the opposite, eastern, flank of the Guards, in order to help seize the bridge at La Forge.

As many as six battalions had now joined the attack, along a front of 2.5 km. Both bridges soon fell. In fact, La Forge was taken even before the 2/Highland Light Infantry arrived. It was the cavalry that secured it. Earlier that morning 2 Cavalry Brigade had reached La Trétoire, only to find the head of the 2nd Division already in action there. It had therefore shifted its attention further east, and towards 12.00 pm managed to force a crossing at La Forge. As for the bridge at Le Gravier, it fell after being outflanked by two companies of the 2/Worcestershire, who, hidden by a bend in the river, waded across near Bécherelle.

Renewed push

Despite having now forced the Petit Morin, the 2nd Division was unable to launch an immediate thrust northwards to the Marne. The dispersed elements of 4 Brigade needed time to reassemble around Boitron on the plateau above the valley. The pause was also necessary for the artillery to come forward from the south side of the Petit Morin, so it could support a renewed push.

It was 2.30 pm before the 2/Grenadiers and 2/Coldstream began to advance across the open country north of Boitron, heading towards the D407, the lateral *chaussée* that ran across their front. To cover their left flank, a battalion from 5 Brigade – the 2/Highland Light Infantry – was pushed north-westwards, from where it could endanger the line of retreat of those German units that were still in the valley further downstream.

Delays ensued when some of the advancing infantry were mis-takenly shelled by their own artillery, and then, towards 4.30 pm, their left rear was suddenly threatened by a German counter-attack. The German troops in question had come from the village of Orly, 2 km west of Boitron. Here, in the valley, three companies of the *Garde-Schützen-Bataillon* had managed to check the 3rd Division (part of II Corps) until the mid-afternoon. One of these companies was a machine-gun company, which began to retreat towards 3.30 pm. Falling back to the north-east, up the wooded slopes, the company reached the top, only to find that it was cut off by the head of the 2nd Division advancing over the plateau further north.

Left with no option but to fight, the *Schützen* opened fire from the edge of the woods with their six machine-guns. British artillery riposted with shrapnel, which felled nearly all the company's horses within moments. Two of the machine-guns also broke down, after the waterjackets that cooled them were shot through. The British infantry completed the company's destruction. The left wing of their foremost line – the 2/Highland Light Infantry and a company of the 2/Coldstream – wheeled round to trap the *Schützen* from the north. At the same time the two rearmost battalions of 4 Brigade – the 3/Coldstream and 1/Irish Guards – launched a direct attack from the area of Boitron. The *Schützen* quickly surrendered, although some managed to escape when British shells burst nearby in yet another incident of friendly fire.

Torrents of rain

The day had become hot and sultry, and a storm was now brewing. At around 5.00 pm the clouds finally broke, unleashing such torrents of rain that it was difficult to see, let alone advance. The rain cleared after about an hour, and that evening 4 and 5 Brigades bivouacked astride the D407. The other brigade, the 6th, had not been engaged, and now passed through to become the advanced guard, halting for the night around La Noue, 5.5 km north of the Petit Morin, and within 2 km of the Marne.

The fighting in the 2nd Division's sector was typical of events that day. The German aim was not to check the BEF – the disparity in numbers would have made that impossible – but to delay it. Simply by forcing the British to halt their march, deploy their long columns and bring forward their howitzers from the rear, the Germans won precious time. The BEF had taken almost an entire day to force its way across the Petit Morin, for in the absence of sufficient firepower it had to rely on manoeuvre. Having deployed advance guards to pin down the Germans and identify weak points, it committed additional infantry brigades to outflank the defences in the valley. Once it had breached the river line at one point, it could easily turn the Germans out of their positions on either flank. This was a long process, taking between five and eight hours, but it eventually succeeded.

British losses were moderate, with the 2nd Division losing 177 officers and men killed, wounded or missing. This reflected the limited numbers of defenders, and the close nature of the terrain. The woods that slowed progress also provided valuable cover for the infantry working their way into the valley. Mistakes were, of course, made. British commanders fed too many battalions into the woods, thereby compounding the confusion. Attempts to outflank the German-held bridges were often belated. Howitzer brigades were too far in the rear of the columns to be available when needed, and during the afternoon poor traffic control allowed the winding road across the valley between La Trétoire and Boitron to become dangerously clogged with transport. Inadequate means of communication between the artillery and infantry caused several friendly-fire incidents.

Even so, the forcing of the Petit Morin shook German morale. 'We were all deeply depressed by this first, great setback in the war', admitted a dragoon. Those units that had been fighting in the valley had found it difficult to break contact when the time came to withdraw. The *Garde-Jäger-Bataillon* lost over a quarter of its strength, and for the *Garde-Kavallerie-Division* it had been the costliest day thus far in the war.

In breaching the line of the Petit Morin, and throwing back the *I Kavallerie-Korps*, the BEF had forced open the gap between the *1.* and *2. Armeen*. That morning, as the pressure mounted, the *I Kavallerie-Korps* had ordered a retreat north-eastwards to the Dolloir river, where it could cover the flank of the *2. Armee*, but only the *Garde-Kavallerie-Division* was able to obey. The other division had to fall back instead to the north, and it retired 10 km behind the Marne. The British had thus split the *I Kavallerie-Korps* into two, causing half of it to withdraw out of their line of advance, and the other half to retreat too far northwards. As a result, much of the BEF would enjoy an unopposed crossing when it reached the even more formidable Marne valley the next day.

WHAT TO SEE

The tour starts at the town of Rebais. To drive there from Meaux, head eastwards along the D603 to La Ferté-sous-Jouarre, and then turn right on to the D204, which leads south-eastwards to Rebais. You can park in the central square, the *place du Marché*.

Point 1: Rebais

Despite its smallness, Rebais is an important road hub. Congestion here delayed the 2nd Division's advance in the morning, and obliged it to bypass the town to the east. In order to follow the division, leave the *place du Marché* by the north-western corner, and

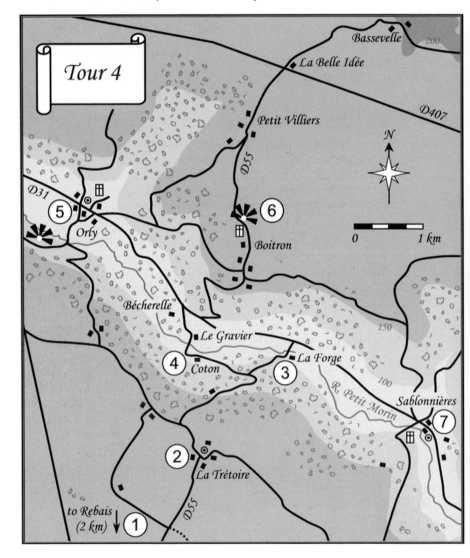

head northwards to the end of the *rue St-Nicolas*. Turn right on to the D204, and then first left up the D222. After 150 metres, when you come to the war memorial, turn off to the left, on to the D55 (signposted for La Trétoire).

Note the nature of the countryside. In places there are extensive views over the fields, but more frequently observation is limited by undulations in the ground, by villages, woods and tree-lined roads. As the BEF advanced, it found traces of abandoned German bivouacs, dead horses fouling the air and countless broken bottles strewn over the ground.

Point 2: La Trétoire
At La Trétoire the advanced guard of the 2nd Division reached the edge of the Petit Morin valley, and came under fire from a German battery on the opposite plateau. The Royal Artillery went into action around the village, and managed to silence the German guns.

La Trétoire. Just beyond the village is the Petit Morin valley.

Go along the D55 as it gently descends through La Trétoire. In the village centre you come to a T-junction. The church is just 50 metres to the right, but to enter the valley turn left (signposted for Boitron). Continue past the left of the war memorial, and after another 150 metres turn right at the crucifix, down the *route de Coton* (the D55). The road now enters the woods of the valley, and begins a steeper, twisting descent. Note the dense undergrowth that helped confuse the attacking units. When you reach the clearing at La Pilloterie (you will see the name on a sign), pause to note the view over the trees to the far side of the valley.

Points 3 and 4: The Petit Morin bridges

So far the D55 has been heading north-eastwards down the slope, but it now loops round to the north-west to continue its descent. Just beyond the loop, take the side-road that branches off to the right. This brings you to the hamlet of La Forge, the more easterly of the two crossing points in the 2nd Division's sector.

Stop here to have a look around. At the time of the battle a railway line used to run along the south bank of the Petit Morin, but this has been dismantled following its closure in 1947. You can still see its route – in this stretch it is followed by a footpath (the *GRP des Morins*). Note that the river at this point actually has two branches, 75 metres apart, and so two bridges had to be taken one after the other. The second was barricaded and covered by German fire from concealed positions on the northern slopes. In the morning a troop of the 4th (Royal Irish) Dragoon Guards tried to take both bridges with a sudden charge directly along the road, but was checked by the barricade, losing five horses killed and two men wounded. It was 12.00 pm before part of the 18th (Queen Mary's Own) Hussars managed to cross further along the river, using a fallen tree trunk. Having thus outflanked La Forge, the hussars helped the 4th Dragoon Guards to take the twin bridges, and part of 4 (Guards) Brigade was then able to cross here.

You will now want to see the other, westerly, crossing point. From La Forge drive back uphill the way you came, until you rejoin the D55. Turn right and descend the road to the hamlet of Coton. Note the large farm immediately north of the Petit Morin here – it was the main stronghold for the *Garde-Jäger* company defending this part of the river. Further to the rear, on the rising slopes of the north side of the valley, the rest of the company was posted behind a series of hedges, so that each of their firing lines overlooked the one in front. But by 11.30 am, when the company finally received the order to retreat, it was so heavily engaged that it had difficulty extracting the platoon holding this farm. Braving the hail of fire, a *Jäger* managed to get through with the order to pull back. The first man to leave was immediately shot through the head, causing the rest to hesitate. Some of the *Jäger* then started singing *O Deutschland hoch in Ehren*, and the others joined in, thus steeling their nerves before they ran from the farm in squads. Up the northern slopes of the valley they dashed, like hares driven by beaters at a hunt, with bullets flying around them. Among the last to leave was the platoon commander, *Oberleutnant Graf* Finckenstein, whose shako flew into the air as it was hit by a bullet. (The *Jäger* wore shakos rather than the spiked helmets of most German infantrymen.)

Just beyond Coton the D55 passes over the bridge at Le Gravier. It was on this western flank that the 2/Worcestershire was fed into the fight in support of the Guards.

Point 5: Orly

The breakthrough near La Trétoire eased the advance of the neighbouring 3rd Division, which had been held up on the left at Orly. We will now make a side-trip to see where it was engaged. From the bridge at Le Gravier, continue along the road until you come to the junction with the D31, and then turn left and drive 2 km down the valley to Orly. Park outside the church, so you can explore the village on foot.

Three companies of the *Garde-Schützen-Bataillon* held Orly. They prepared the village for defence, opening fields of fire and digging dummy trenches to distract the British from the real trenches, which were further back in a shady, roadside ditch. To complete the deception, the *Schützen* added some of their shakos to the dummy positions.

The 3rd Division's advanced guard – 8 Brigade – attacked Orly frontally, and two battalions of 9 Brigade were inserted on the right flank in the afternoon. Casualties among the *Garde-Schützen* gradually mounted. Men grew thirsty in the blazing heat of the day, but the intense firing prevented them from fetching water. It was 3.15 pm before they finally received the order to retreat, and by then it was too late to slip away without heavy loss. At around 4.30 pm the last of the rearguard fell back, and the British were finally able to enter Orly from the south.

The defence by the *Schützen* had been compromised by British crossings of the river on either flank. To the east, the 2nd Division had sent elements of 5 Brigade towards Orly along the D31, led by a platoon of 2/Connaught Rangers. To the west, the 5th Division had crossed at St-Ouen, and then pushed its cyclist company along the road leading northwards out of the valley. Reaching the lateral *chaussée* (the D407), the cyclists turned to the east, and cut off 150 of the retreating *Schützen*. But they were then peppered with shrapnel from their own artillery, and fired on by British infantry advancing

The British view of Orly. The Germans held the village, and positions on either side, but dug dummy trenches to distract their attackers.

from the south, and lost more than half their prisoners amid the confusion.

For a good view of Orly from the British side of the Petit Morin, head south along the *rue de la Borde* from immediately west of the church. After crossing the bridge over the river, you come to a fork in the road. Take the road on the right (the V2, or *rue de la Montagne blanche*, signposted for Gibraltar and Rebais). It climbs uphill through the trees, which then clear on the right to give you an excellent viewpoint.

Return to the centre of Orly to visit the local cemetery. From the church, walk south-eastwards along the D31 for 50 metres, until (just before you come to a bridge over a stream) you see a signpost on the left for the *cimitière*. Follow the sign, up the *rue des Picards*, and after 175 metres you will be level with the cemetery. It lies almost 50 metres on the left of the road and is easy to miss, as the turning is not signposted.

On entering the cemetery you will see a Commonwealth War Graves Commission plot on the left. The headstones do not mark actual graves. Instead the soldiers are buried in a vault beneath the *commune*'s own war memorial. Four of the stones are identified as those of Captain Anthony Morris Coats Hewat of the 2/Royal Scots, and three privates of the 2/Royal Irish Regiment. These two regiments belonged to 8 Brigade, which attacked Orly from the south. Captain Hewat was killed whilst directing fire. Aged 29, he left a wife and a one-year-old daughter.

Point 6: Boitron

Retrieve your car, drive along the D31 to the eastern exit of Orly, and then take the V4 (signposted for Boitron), which leads diagonally up the northern slopes of the valley. Ignore the turning to the left inside the wood (it leads to Petit Villiers), and instead continue into Boitron at the top of the plateau. Turn left at the T-junction by the war memorial, and drive northwards along the *route du Moncet*. When you come to the end of the village, stop at the cemetery. This was where Boitron church stood at the time of the battle, but it has since been demolished. Inside the cemetery, in the north-western corner, are five Commonwealth graves. The three that have been identified

The view from Boitron cemetery. The machine-guns of the **Garde-Schützen** *opened fire from the woods on the left.*

are those of Privates Mark Lockwood and Albert Teesdale of the 3/Coldstream, and Private G. Shannon of the 2/Worcestershire.

From the cemetery the view extends northwards over the scene of the final phase of the action, as 4 Brigade advanced across the fields towards the D407. Note the proximity of the cemetery to the woods further north-west, from where the machine-guns of the *Garde-Schützen-Bataillon* opened fire. Sir Douglas Haig himself witnessed the defeat of this threat. Having crossed the Petit Morin at Sablonnières at around 2.00 pm, he rode his horse to Boitron, where he found the Royal Artillery firing furiously at the woods. He went to confer with the commander of the 2nd Division, who was at the church. The British batteries around Boitron had moved forwards from across the valley to support the advance. On being shot at from the woods, some of the artillerymen turned their guns in that direction, whilst others actually seized their rifles and charged the wood, taking several prisoners.

Point 7: Sablonnières
From Boitron head southwards down the D55 as it snakes its way into the Petit Morin valley. Turn left when you reach the T-junction with the D31, and drive along the valley to Sablonnières, 4 km to the south-east. Immediately after passing the *mairie*, turn right and park at the church. Sablonnières has two local cemeteries, having opened a new one after the first became full. You should visit the older one. To reach it, walk back along the D31 until you are near the war memorial at the north-western outskirts of the village. Turn left on to the D222 (signposted for Rebais and La Ferté-Gaucher). Follow it across the Petit Morin and after another 150 metres, where the road bends to the left, you will come to the cemetery.

Nineteen British soldiers are buried here, all of whom fell on 8 September. They include two officers of the 5th (Princess Charlotte of Wales's) Dragoon Guards, both of whom were veterans of the South African War. Captain Robert Partridge commanded C Squadron, while 38-year-old Captain John Norwood was serving in B Squadron. Norwood had won the Victoria Cross in South Africa fifteen years earlier.

The 5th Dragoon Guards helped cover the advance of the 1st Division, which formed the BEF's easternmost column. Since the Germans held Sablonnières, Partridge and Norwood were ordered to outflank them by crossing the Petit Morin 2.5 km to the south-east at Bellot with five troops of their regiment. They found that part of a French cavalry division had already seized the bridge at Bellot, but without being able to push further north. Thus, instead of crossing the river to attack Sablonnières along the far bank, Partridge and Norwood moved along the southern side of the river, intending to fire at Sablonnières from the flank. But the plan miscarried, for they themselves came under heavy fire in an exposed meadow some 800 metres short of the village. Both of them were killed, along with Privates Bert Wisdom and Oliver Fishlock, who are also buried in the cemetery.

Captain Norwood.

The deed that won Norwood the VC. In October 1899 he came under fire whilst on patrol, and in riding away saw one of his men topple from the saddle. He galloped back, dismounted and carried the man to safety.

The survivors were now pinned down. More firepower was belatedly deployed in support, including machine-guns and a couple of artillery pieces. But the decisive move was an infantry attack along the north bank of the Petit Morin, using the approach that Partridge and Norwood had been unable to take earlier that morning. The leading battalion of the 1st Division – the 1/Black Watch – had now reached Bellot, and passed through the French cavalry to secure the northern slopes of the valley. B Company moved down the river towards Sablonnières, and it was during this attack that its commander was shot through the lung. Another of its officers, Captain Charles de Guerry Dalglish, was mortally wounded, so Lieutenant Ewen Wilson took command, only to be killed soon afterwards. (Both Wilson and Dalglish are buried at Sablonnières cemetery.) B Company was reinforced by more of the Black Watch, and by part of the 1/Cameron Highlanders, and this combined force managed to clear the Germans from their positions east of Sablonnières. Towards 1.00 pm the defenders finally abandoned the village, leaving around fifty prisoners in British hands.

Optional visit

The tour ends at Sablonnières, but you may wish to visit the little village of Bassevelle, 6 km to the north, as you drive back to your base. Just inside the churchyard is the grave of Lieutenant Reginald Johnstone of the 1/Cameron Highlanders, who fell during the attack on Sablonnières. His grave is particularly poignant, since he had married less than two months earlier, and he left a widow, Honoria, who was only 19. She remarried a couple of years later but died in 1929, aged 33. She was the granddaughter of a most remarkable character, Walter James Hore-Ruthven, 8th Baron Ruthven, a veteran of the Crimea who nonetheless managed to serve in the First World War six decades later. Having joined the Rifle Brigade in 1854, he rose to the rank of major before retiring in 1886. For the next quarter of a century he led a sedate life, pursuing his hobbies of fishing and gardening, until everything was suddenly turned upside down by the death of his wife and the outbreak of the First World War. Now aged 76, he insisted on returning to duty with the Rifle Brigade at its depot in Winchester. In 1915 he was appointed a King's Messenger – a diplomatic courier for important documents – and frequently crossed the English Channel. During one of these visits to France he caused a minor flap by going missing. 'Where is Lord Ruthven?' demanded the BEF's General Headquarters in telegraphs sent across northern France. It turned out that he had taken the opportunity to visit a trench right on the front line, where he spent the night in a sap in the hope of sniping a German at dawn.

Tour 5

FORCING THE MARNE

This tour follows the BEF's advance across the Marne on 9 September, the day that marked the climax of the battle. We shall focus on the western wing, which was the only part of the BEF to run into significant opposition. Exploring this sector reveals a key reason for the slowness of the British advance: the hilly, intricate terrain is a stark contrast to the open, rolling plateau of the Battlefield of the Ourcq just 15–20 km further west.

WHAT HAPPENED

The BEF had been obliged to fight its way across the Petit Morin on the 8th, and expected to have to repeat the process the next day at the even more formidable obstacle of the Marne. For the Germans, the Marne would have been an ideal defensive position, without the disadvantages they had found on the Petit Morin. Quite apart from being a major river, some 60–80 metres wide, it lay in a broad and deep valley. Thickly wooded heights on the north bank offered cover from where artillery and machine-guns might sweep the exposed valley floor that the British would have to cross.

Yet the Germans, incredibly, did not attempt to defend the line of the Marne on most of the BEF's front. The simple truth is that they had run out of time to try to do so. On the 8th the *1. Armee* had detached two infantry regiments and six artillery batteries to cover its rear against the threat posed by the BEF. Commanded by *Generalmajor* Richard von Kraewel, this composite brigade was intended to block the British advance at the Marne, but was unable to assemble its units around the town of Montreuil-aux-Lions before the evening. Kraewel decided to remain at Montreuil for the night, as his troops were too tired to march immediately to the Marne, some 6 or 8 km to

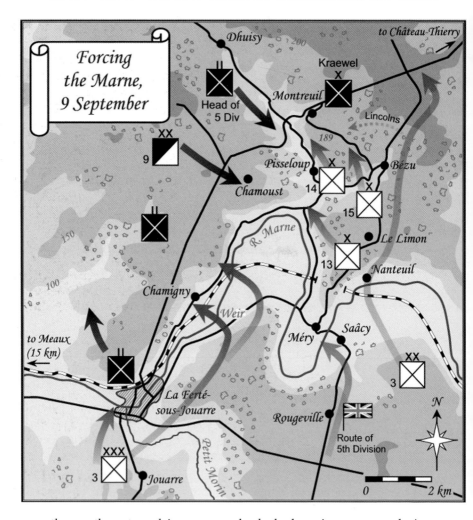

Forcing
the Marne,
9 September

to Château-Thierry

Dhuisy

Kraewel

Head of
5 Div

Montreuil

Lincolns

Pisseloup

Chamoust

14

Bézu

15

R. Marne

Le Limon

13

Nanteuil

Chamigny

Weir

Méry

Saâcy

to Meaux
(15 km)

3

La Ferté-
sous-Jouarre

Rougeville

Route of
5th Division

N

3

Jouarre

Petit Morin

0   2 km

the south-east, and in any case he lacked engineers or explosives with which to blow up its bridges.

Since the BEF resumed its advance early on the morning of the 9th, it found the bridges east of La Ferté-sous-Jouarre not only intact but undefended. (Only at La Ferté-sous-Jouarre itself were the bridges broken – the British themselves had blown them up five days earlier to cover their retreat from Mons.) Thus, the British right and centre – I and II Corps – were able to cross the Marne and secure the high

The main bridge at La Ferté-sous-Jouarre.

ground overlooking the river without any significant resistance. It was still only 9.00 am, and we know with hindsight that a vigorous thrust to the north might have crushed part of the *1. Armee* on the Ourcq. Yet at the time it was the risk in striking out so boldly that seemed more obvious to the BEF's commanders. Aerial reconnaissance ought to have relieved some of these fears, but on this occasion proved a mixed blessing. That morning the Royal Flying Corps spotted strong German forces on the BEF's eastern flank. In reality, these units were transport columns and a cavalry division intent only on vacating the area, but their presence caused alarm that the BEF might be caught by a powerful counter-attack while still straddling the Marne.

The alarm caused the advance of I Corps in the east to be suspended until 3.00 pm while the situation was clarified. In the centre II Corps ground to a halt in the afternoon when one of its two divisions – the 5th Division – ran into Kraewel's brigade near Montreuil. On the western wing III Corps made even less progress, being checked at La Ferté-sous-Jouarre. By the end of 9 September the British had nowhere penetrated more than 10 km north of the Marne. Yet despite the hesitant nature of their advance, they had posed enough of a threat to the rear of the *1. Armee* to provoke a German retreat.

The 5th Division

We begin the tour by examining the 5th Division's passage of the Marne. Its advanced guard (14 Brigade) set off at 4.45 am, and crossed the river without opposition at Saâcy. Barely 7 km now separated it from the lateral *chaussée* between La Ferté-sous-Jouarre and Château-Thierry, but Kraewel was straddling that road at the town of Montreuil. To the south-west he was supported by two divisions of the *II Kavallerie-Korps*, which held the line of the Marne from near Chamigny westwards to the mouth of the Ourcq. At the central point of Montreuil, Kraewel could cover the line of retreat of those German forces around La Ferté-sous-Jouarre, while also posing a threat to the flank of any northward push by British formations to the east of him.

Hence the 5th Division found the next stage of its advance altogether more difficult. By 8.00 am the head of 14 Brigade had climbed the northern slopes of the Marne valley, and occupied the high ground at Le Limon that dominated the river and its bridges. It had thereby secured the crossings, but now came under German shellfire. One of Kraewel's batteries – the 6th Battery of *Feldartillerie-Regiment Nr 45* – could be seen at Hill 189 (part of Pisseloup ridge), 3.25 km to the north-west. It was soon silenced, but other German batteries were in concealed positions that proved difficult to locate.

The 5th Division faced a particularly challenging task, for as well as running into German opposition to the front, it found itself threatened from the west. The problem was that the Marne wound its way through the countryside in great loops. Since III Corps was checked at La Ferté-sous-Jouarre, at the southern end of a loop, the neighbouring 5th Division would find its western flank becoming more and more exposed as it pushed forwards.

At 10.00 am 14 Brigade resumed its advance from Le Limon, heading for Montreuil, 4 km to the north-west. To escape the worst of the German shrapnel fire, it avoided the open plateau north of Le Limon, and instead moved through the woods that covered the slopes on its western side. Dense undergrowth slowed progress, obliging a section of the Royal Engineers to cut a narrow track through the thickets.

Meanwhile, the head of the other division of II Corps, the 3rd Division, had crossed the Marne at Nanteuil, and occupied Bézu, on the 5th Division's right flank. At 10.30 am half of one of its battalions, the 1/Lincolns, was sent through the *Bois des Essertis* to make a surprise attack from the east against the German battery at Hill 189. It managed to capture the guns, but then had to fall back.

By 11.30 am 14 Brigade had made its way through 2 km of woodland and emerged on to the D16, a lateral road at the bottom of a valley cutting across its line of advance. From this valley the brigade faced an uphill climb to the top of the next piece of high ground,

The 1/Lincolns attack the German battery at Hill 189.

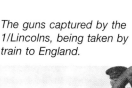

The guns captured by the 1/Lincolns, being taken by train to England.

the Pisseloup ridge, which extended 1.5 km to the north-west and then ended above the town of Montreuil. Much of the ridge was thickly wooded, and the western slopes were covered with vineyards. This slowed the advance, and made it difficult for units to remain in touch with each other. The Germans had dug trenches on top of the ridge – on either side of the road running from Montreuil to Bézu – from where they were able to fire into the eastern flank of 14 Brigade's advance. The trenches were skilfully arranged so that the British could not attack one trench without exposing their flank to fire from another. At the same time the advance was enfiladed on the other side by German artillery concealed on the high ground near Chamoust, some 2 km to the west.

Shortly after 2.00 pm 15 Brigade joined the attack on Pisseloup ridge. The intention was to extend 14 Brigade's attack eastwards, and thus outflank the German entrenchments. But by 4.00 pm 15 Brigade, too, had been checked. The heavily wooded terrain and the scarcity of suitable firing positions prevented the British artillery from lending direct support by firing at the German infantry positions and their machine-guns. As a result, the attackers were pinned down in an intense firefight, unable to manoeuvre or even to pull back until nightfall.

German threat

On the 5th Division's left flank a new threat was emerging. The *II Kavallerie-Korps* had concentrated on the high ground 7 km west of Montreuil. Just after noon its commander, *General der Kavallerie* Georg von der Marwitz, ordered an attack. His *9. Kavallerie-Division*, advancing past Chamoust, was to assail the 5th Division's western flank. In addition, part of the German *5. Infanterie-Division* had been pulled out of the Battle of the Ourcq, and was now marching eastwards to reinforce the hard-pressed Kraewel.

In the event, this powerful counter-thrust never properly materialized, for the German commanders were distracted by exaggerated reports of threats developing on either of their flanks – by the 3rd Division apparently outflanking Montreuil to the east, and elements of III Corps managing to force the Marne to the south-west. Instead of launching a single, powerful onslaught into the flank of the 5th Division, the Germans ended up simply containing its advance until nightfall. Only the leading battalion of their *5. Infanterie-Division* ever came into action. During the afternoon it pushed forward from the vicinity of Montreuil, against the village of Pisseloup and the left flank of 14 Brigade, but was soon checked. Attempts by the *9. Kavallerie-Division* to attack were repeatedly suspended because of the lack of clarity about the overall situation. The Germans found it no easier than the British to locate the opposing artillery in such terrain, and so any advance they made was quickly smothered by shrapnel.

Nonetheless, the 5th Division continued to be annoyed by the enfilade fire from the German guns near Chamoust. In order to counter the threat from this area, two battalions of 13 Brigade were inserted on the left of 14 Brigade. They pushed along the bottom of the Marne valley (the river here forms a loop projecting north-wards), past Courcelles and Caumont. By dusk the leading battalion had occupied the top of the hill above the village of Moitiébard without opposition, and thus secured the 5th Division's left flank. The advance made it possible for an artillery officer on reconnais-sance to pinpoint the location of a German battery concealed in the

A German battery.

woods, thus allowing its troublesome fire to be silenced by British howitzers.

Darkness brought the action to a close, and enabled the Germans to break contact and retreat. The II Corps has been criticized for not deploying more of its strength to achieve a breakthrough, yet what was really needed was artillery support. Unfortunately, it proved difficult to locate the German guns, even when suitable firing positions could be found. At this early stage in the war batteries tended to come into action individually, rather than as part of a plan that concentrated the firepower of several divisions, as that would have required means of communication that were not yet available. In the absence of radio links, battery commanders also struggled to keep track of how far the infantry had progressed, which explains the frequency of friendly fire.

The passage of the Marne has an added interest because it reveals the speed at which the Royal Flying Corps (RFC) was evolving. Just two years old, the RFC was keen to develop its full potential, and one of the innovations it made at this time was to decentralize its reconnaissance in order to speed up the reporting of information. Starting during the Battle of the Marne, a flight from an RFC squadron was attached to each of I and II Corps. Instead of flying back to the RFC base, the airplanes would land at a temporary ground to report directly to the corps, or would even drop written reports from the air. On 9 September the flight attached to II Corps flew reconnaissances throughout the day, to ascertain which bridges remained intact on the Marne, to locate the German positions and to keep track of the neighbouring corps' progress. The airmen's efforts were not helped when they were mistakenly fired on by their own troops. At the time of the battle their wings bore not the familiar roundel of today but the Union Jack, which from the ground could be difficult to distinguish from the black crosses of German airplanes.

WHAT TO SEE

The tour starts at the village of Rougeville, 2.5 km south of the Marne, where the head of the 5th Division spent the night of 8/9 September. To reach it from Meaux, drive eastwards along the D603, through the southern part of La Ferté-sous-Jouarre, and continue eastwards

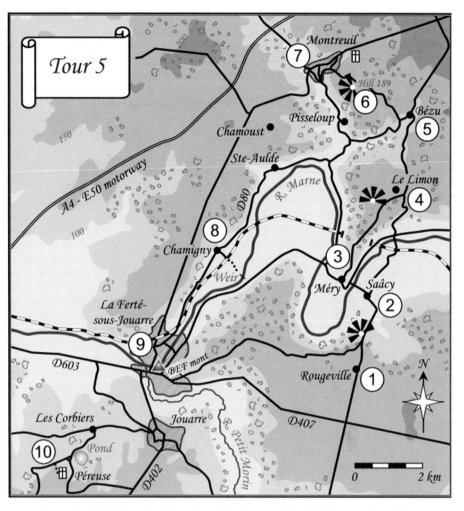

along the D407 in the direction of Montmirail. At Montapeine, 6 km
from La Ferté-sous-Jouarre, turn left on to the D68. Rougeville lies
1.5 km along this road.

Point 1: Rougeville
Drive through Rougeville, along the D68 (signposted for Saâcy). To
the north of the village you soon begin the descent into the Marne
valley, and enter a belt of trees, inside which the D70 joins the road

you are on from the left. Immediately after passing this junction, park on the little strip of gravel on the left-hand side of the road. Walk to the end of the strip, where the belt of trees comes to an end, and you will be able to look right across to the heights on the far side of the Marne. This was the view that greeted Captain Robert Dolbey of the Royal Army Medical Corps, who was near the tail of the 5th Division. As he waited here, Dolbey watched the action unfold on the opposite side of the valley. 'A beautiful sight it was to see our mounted men and guns work up the slopes in front of us', he wrote.

> They seemed to take the steep ascent at a gallop, unmindful of the fleecy clouds of cotton wool that were the enemy shrapnel. The gunners unlimbered at the edge of a wood and in a cornfield that bounded the fringe of trees on the

The view from near Rougeville.

south side. We could clearly see them running to bring sheaves of corn to screen the guns from view. Then the red tongues of flame stabbed the green background of the wood, as they shelled the German transport on the reverse slopes of the hill. But the cavalry suffered from the shrapnel fire; and, often, we could see little groups of riderless horses tearing down the slope of open ground to the river below; and the tiny figures of dismounted men trying to head them back.

The Marne was one of the last great battles in which it was possible to behold such scenes. The first weeks of the war, before the two sides became dug in all along the Western Front, saw a curious mixture of the old and the new. In some sectors the firepower of modern weapons made the battlefield seem empty, as troops sought whatever cover they could find. Elsewhere, it seemed nearer to a Napoleonic clash, being filled with movement and even, in the case of the French army, with brightly coloured uniforms. For almost the last time in Europe, an army commander was able to watch the progress of the fighting in person, and along the stretch of road where you are standing a whole succession of generals passed to and fro in motorcars on 9 September, including Sir John French, Sir Horace Smith-Dorrien of II Corps and the commander of the 5th Division, Sir Charles Fergusson.

Point 2: Saâcy

Follow the D68 down into the valley and into Saâcy. When you come to a no-through-road sign, turn to the right, following the signpost for the *centre ville*. This brings you to a roundabout, the *Rond pont du centre*. Take the third right, for a brief look around the centre of Saâcy. Then return to the roundabout, and head down the D68a (signposted for Château-Thierry, Nanteuil-sur-Marne, and La Ferté-sous-Jouarre).

Point 3: Méry

Some 500 metres from Saâcy the road crosses the Marne. Immediately afterwards, turn left on to the D402 (signposted for Méry). This leads round a bend to the southern side of Méry. Immediately after the bend, enter the village by taking the first right (it is easy to miss, for the street has only a discreet sign identifying it as the *Grande rue*). Turn right again up the *rue de l'Ecole*, and drive along it to the church at the end, where you can usually find a parking space.

The church housed some of the wounded who flowed back from the fighting further north. All three of the 5th Division's field ambulance units spent the night of 9/10 September near the Marne bridge. Stretcher-bearers and ambulance waggons collected injured soldiers, and brought them back so their wounds could be dressed by the surgeons. On the morning of the 10th the field ambulances sent off the men in their care by road to Coulommiers, a railhead 20 km to the south, and then left the Marne valley to search for the remaining wounded in the terrain further north.

Point 4: Le Limon

From Méry drive north-eastwards up the *Grande rue*, which becomes the *route du Limon* after leaving the village. This steep, narrow road was the route taken on the morning of the 9th by 14 Brigade – the advanced guard of the 5th Division – after it had crossed the Marne. Having ascended a long, wooded spur, the road reaches the top of the plateau, and emerges from the trees near the hamlet of Le Limon.

When 14 Brigade reached this point, it came under German shellfire. For the next stage of its advance – northwards, in the direction of Montreuil – it therefore avoided this exposed terrain and moved instead under the cover of the woods you can see to the west and north-west. The drawback was that the paucity of tracks through the dense undergrowth slowed the advance. In the wake of 14 Brigade came the Reverend Owen Watkins with a party of stretcher-bearers. Watkins wrote:

> What was happening it was difficult to discover, for the trees hid everything from our view. Like ceaseless thunder there came to us the noise of the guns; above was the deep hum of a German aeroplane, of which we got occasional glimpses through the tangled branches overhead; once and again the sudden rip-rip-rip of a machine gun – the infantry had come to a gap in the trees, and were letting the enemy have it. And silently, in single file, the regiments

View from the plateau near Le Limon.

worked their way through the trees, down a steep hill, up another, until the shell[s] were passing our heads – it seemed that, screened by the thicket, we had advanced nearer to the enemy's lines than they realized.

To obtain the best view from the open ground at Le Limon, you need to stop the car and walk a couple of hundred metres along a track that branches off into the fields on the left of the road. The start of this track lies 200 metres north-east of the point where you emerged from the woods. As you head along it, you gain an extensive view of the terrain to the north, including Bézu village, the next point on this tour.

Point 5: Bézu

After returning to your car, continue driving along the road. At the T-junction 200 metres beyond the hamlet of Le Limon, turn left (signposted for Bézu). After 2.5 km you come to the southern houses

Captain Drake.

of Bézu. Continue straight ahead, through these outskirts, and then turn left on to the D16, which leads you round to the village centre. Park at the church and walk from the adjacent roundabout to the local cemetery, you will find 200 metres to the north-east along the D84. Near the cemetery entrance is a cluster of graves of the 1/Lincolns, the unit that surprised the battery of *Feldartillerie-Regiment Nr 45* at Hill 189. They include the Adjutant, Captain Robert Drake, whose date of death is wrongly recorded as 8 September. In fact, he was mortally wounded on the 9th, and died shortly after being found in the woods the next morning.

Point 6: Hill 189

From Bézu church drive westwards through the village, along the D16. Pass the local war memorial and then, 150 metres further on, turn right as you leave Bézu. The turning is easy to miss, being marked only by a faded signpost for Montreuil. (Don't go straight ahead – that road is also signposted for Montreuil, but is longer and less interesting.)

As you drive north-westwards, you soon find the trees of the *Bois des Essertis* alongside you on the right. The wood then recedes away from the road and after another 400 metres you reach high ground with extensive views to the west and south. This is Hill 189. It was an obvious point for the Germans to entrench, as it dominates the approaches to the low-lying town of Montreuil. (The altitude of 189 metres is taken from the map used by the BEF in 1914, and differs slightly from that indicated on modern maps.)

It was in the vicinity of Hill 189 that two companies of the 1/Lincolns surprised the German battery. As they worked their way towards the western edge of the *Bois des Essertis*, they could hear the sound of the guns. One of the company commanders, Captain Henry Hoskyns, neared the last of the trees and saw the battery barely 140 metres away. He had come up against its left flank, but was aghast to see a German sentry staring in his direction from a distance of a few metres. Hoskyns froze. At last the man turned and began walking away, but then stopped, and once again looked towards him, as if he realized something was amiss. The Lincolns now opened fire, catching the gunners by surprise before they could turn the guns round in their direction. They then ran forward to seize the battery, only to be counter-attacked by a German infantry company; they were also fired on by some distant British gunners who mistook them for the foe. The Lincolns had to fall back through the *Bois des Essertis*, leaving the battery behind. Later that day the Germans tried three times to save the guns by bringing forward the limbers, but were foiled by the intensity of fire and had to abandon them when they retreated after dusk.

Point 7: Montreuil-aux-Lions

Now drive the final 1 km along the road to Montreuil. When the British finally occupied this little town on 10 September, they used the *mairie* as a temporary hospital. Stretcher-bearers scoured the woods where the fighting had taken place the day before, and brought the remaining wounded to the hospital. At the same time the dead were buried. The Reverend Owen Watkins was serving with the 14th Field Ambulance. He wrote:

> In field, garden, orchard, and vineyard – just where they had fallen – we laid the dead to rest. Sometimes a single man, sometimes two or three together. But at last we reached the hilltop crowned with trees [Pisseloup ridge], and here we found signs of a fight almost beyond belief – such a hurricane of lead had passed through the wood that there did not appear to be a tree-trunk unscarred by it. Here our dead lay thick – Surrey, Manchester, Suffolk, Dorset, and Cornishmen; in one grave we buried two officers and eighteen men, and altogether we buried forty-one.

After the armistice of 1918 these various graves were removed to a newly created British military cemetery at the eastern exit of Montreuil. To reach it, drive past the church, follow the *rue de l'Eglise* round to the right, and continue down the slope to the T-junction. Turn right on to the *avenue de Paris* (the D1003), and go up it to the cemetery on the right – you can stop in the little car-parking area at the roadside. Normally, fallen British soldiers were left where they were originally buried, but in some cases, as happened here, the dead were moved so that their graves could be more easily maintained. This is why Montreuil is one of only two Commonwealth War Graves Commission cemeteries to contain a large number of British dead from the Battle of the Marne. The other is at Perreuse *Château*, which we will visit at the end of this tour.

Note the grave of 26-year-old Lieutenant Lionel Woodgate, of the 1/King's Own (Royal Lancaster Regiment), at the southern end of the cemetery (Plot IV, Row B, Grave 1). He was the nephew of Major-General Sir Edward Woodgate, who had been mortally wounded at Spion Kop in 1900, during the South African War. His battalion belonged to III Corps, on the left wing of the BEF, and he fell on 8 September while trying to clear the town of La Ferté-sous-Jouarre. He was leading a party of men towards a bridge in the north-eastern part of the town, but was shot when he reached a square exposed to German observation from the opposite bank of the Marne. A handful of volunteers dashed forward to bring him back, but were themselves caught in a sudden burst of fire. Two of them – Corporal James Pike and Private Stanley Everson – are buried just a short distance from Woodgate, the officer they tried to rescue (Plot III, Row C, Graves 1 and 2).

In the rest of this tour we will visit the area around La Ferté-sous-Jouarre. Whereas II and I Corps found the Marne bridges in their sectors practically undefended, and ran into resistance, if at all, only in the hills further north, III Corps had to force a passage of the river. It had managed to enter La Ferté-sous-Jouarre on the afternoon of the 8th, and had cleared the part of the town that lay on the south bank of the Marne. But the presence of a *Jäger* battalion across the river made 9 September a frustrating day: with both of the town's bridges destroyed, it was impossible to force a passage within La Ferté-sous-Jouarre while the *Jäger* still held the houses on the far bank. Dislodging the defenders took both an artillery bombardment and the threat of envelopment, with III Corps managing to slip four battalions round to the right, to pass the Marne between 2 and 5 km upstream of the town. Towards evening, work began on building a floating bridge within La Ferté-sous-Jouarre itself, but it would take another day for the remainder of III Corps to cross to the north bank.

Point 8: Chamigny

From the cemetery at Montreuil drive back down the D1003, through the town, and at the bottom of the hill, just before the road bends round to the left over the bridge, turn left on to the *rue de Pisseloup* (the D16). Continue through Pisseloup, and then turn right on to the D80 (signposted for La Ferté-sous-Jouarre). After 1 km you will come to another road junction near Caumont, but continue along the D80 (signposted for Ste-Aulde), over the little bridge. On your right is the hillside climbed by part of 13 Brigade in the evening. Follow the D80 along the right bank of the Marne, through Moitiébard and Ste-Aulde, until you reach the village of Chamigny. It was here that a detachment of III Corps managed to establish a bridgehead by boldly attacking across a weir and its adjoining lock – the *barrage* and *écluse de Courtaron*.

To reach the scene of this feat, we will walk the 1 km down to the river. (Driving there is possible, but involves passing along a track.) Park in the centre of Chamigny and then, walking from the *mairie* south-westwards down the D80, take the first left. (It is easy to over-shoot the turning, as the streetname – the *rue de la Marne* – is not visible from the D80. If you pass the church, then you have gone too far.) The *rue de la Marne* leads south-eastwards and after 250 metres becomes a dirt track that runs along the left-hand side of a large farm called the *Ferme de Godefroy*. It then passes over the railway line and 300 metres further on comes to a crossroads. Continue straight ahead, along the less well-used track, and on reaching the riverbank follow it round to the left until you see the weir.

The purpose of the weir is to keep the river navigable even during the dry season. It has been modernized since 1914, but the basic layout remains the same – a footbridge over the top, and a lock alongside to enable boats to pass. The footbridge is out of bounds, so if you wish to see the far bank you will need to drive all the way round through La Ferté-sous-Jouarre – a distance of 7 km.

The weir was an obvious place for III Corps to try to force the Marne, thereby outflanking the German troops who were defending

NE

Lock-keeper's cottage

2/Essex attack across open ground

Lock

Weir

Marne river flowing towards La Ferté-sous-Jouarre

The weir at Chamigny today.

La Ferté-sous-Jouarre. Two battalions were sent on this outflanking mission – the 2/Essex and 2/Lancashire Fusiliers. The woods on the eastern bank covered the approach of their advanced guard ('D' Company of the 2/Essex, under Major Frederick Moffitt) to within 200 metres. But from there an attack would have to cross the exposed meadows to reach the lock-keeper's house, before passing the Marne itself – some 75 metres wide at this point – followed by almost 1 km of open ground to Chamigny. Nobody knew whether any Germans were present.

A party of eight men dashed forward under Sergeant William Sharpley. The embanked track leading to the weir provided some cover, but two of the party were shot and wounded. The firing had come from a copse at the western end of the weir, but was immediately smothered by four machine-guns that had been established at the edge of the woods to cover the attack from either flank. A few German soldiers were seen fleeing to the rear, and one of

Sharpley's party returned to guide two platoons to the lock by the least exposed route.

The only people inside the house on the east bank were the lock-keeper and his wife. Major Moffitt now led his men in single-file across first the lock-gates and then the narrow footbridge above the weir. Only one German remained on the far bank, and he was dead. The bold stroke had secured a bridgehead at a cost of just two casualties. By the end of the day four battalions had passed the river either at the weir or by the railway bridge 1.5 km further north at Le Saussoy.

Point 9: La Ferté-sous-Jouarre

To reach La Ferté-sous-Jouarre, return to your car and drive from Chamigny along the D80, which will bring you into the town centre. You will want to spend an hour or two walking around here, so try parking at the railway station, or else at the *Hôtel de ville*, which holds the register of names for the town's BEF Monument (see below).

The importance of La Ferté-sous-Jouarre lay in its proximity to the Battlefield of the Ourcq just 15 km to the west. This was why III Corps ran into such opposition at the town. It managed to clear the houses on the south bank of the Marne on the afternoon of the 8th, but for most of the next day was blocked by the Germans holding the rest of the town on the far side of the river. By delaying the British passage here, the Germans were able to win enough time for the southern wing of their *1. Armee* on the Ourcq to retreat out of danger.

You will find the main points of interest on the south bank. A couple of bridges link the two parts of the town, and are just out of sight from each other round a bend in the Marne. From the main (eastern) bridge, look downstream. Note the large white supermarket on the left bank – at the time of writing, it has the name of the Leader Price chain in red letters on the front. Head towards it by turning right at the end of the bridge, and walking along the *quai des Anglais*. When you reach the supermarket's car-park, turn away from the river and go along the front of the supermarket until you reach the next street. At the corner house are two privately erected memorials to Second Lieutenant Edward James Vibart Collingwood-

Thompson, of the 2/Royal Welch Fusiliers – a plaque on the wall, and a stone marking the spot where he fell mortally wounded on the morning of 9 September. The street had been full of soldiers wandering about, or brewing tea, when they suddenly came under machine-gun fire from across the river. Collingwood-Thompson was just 20 years old, and we will visit his grave at the final stop in this tour.

Second Lieutenant Collingwood-Thompson.

Collingwood-Thompson's monument in La Ferté-sous-Jouarre.

Return past the supermarket to the Marne, turn left and walk alongside the river for another 350 metres until you come to the BEF Monument, at the point where the D603 joins the D407.

BEF Monument
The monument has a dual role: it commemorates the BEF's operations up to mid-October 1914, and honours almost 4,000 fallen from that opening phase of the war who have no known grave. It was unveiled in November 1928 by Lieutenant General Sir William Pulteney, the former commander of III Corps, with a guard of honour composed of veterans of 1914 from every regiment or corps of the original BEF.

The question of how to commemorate the missing caused much soul-searching in Britain after the war. Recording their names at whichever military cemetery was closest to the place they had fallen was ruled out, since it was impossible to ascertain exactly where all of them had been killed. The solution was to have just a handful of memorials to the missing, each covering a broad area. This concept then became fused with a separate idea, that of erecting impressive, national monuments for the key battles. The number of planned

BEF Monument.

memorials on the Western Front with this dual function of commemorating both a battle and the missing was eventually reduced to just four, all of which were unveiled between 1927 and 1932. The Thiepval Memorial on the Somme (over 72,000 missing) and the Menin Gate at Ypres (over 54,000 missing) are the largest and most famous, yet those at La Ferté-sous-Jouarre and Neuve-Chapelle (the latter commemorating almost 5,000 missing of the Army of India) are also unique and memorable.

It was Sir John French who recommended La Ferté-sous-Jouarre as the location for the 1914 monument. Other senior officers suggested Troyon on the Battlefield of the Aisne, Messines near Ypres, or Givenchy in northern France. That these alternatives were proposed is understandable, since of all the BEF's principal battles in 1914 the Marne was the least bloody and the least arduous. Yet the Marne was Germany's first major defeat in the west, and La Ferté-sous-Jouarre was easily accessible for visitors, unlike some rural areas far from Paris. For the British, the bridging of the Marne at this point marked the culmination of the battle, and the stage at which they ceased having to fight their way forward and began a pursuit.

The missing are listed by regiment. At the rear of the monument, on Panel 21, look for Private Thomas James Highgate, of the 1/Queen's Own (Royal West Kent Regiment). The inclusion of his name is particularly interesting, since he was actually executed for desertion on 8 September, while the battle was being fought. His execution was part of a general tightening-up of discipline following the end of the retreat from Mons. He was, in fact, the first British soldier in the First World War to be executed under the Army Act. The controversy over Highgate's fate focuses not so much on whether he was guilty of trying to desert – there is little doubt that he was – but on whether he should have been given a lesser punishment. He was discovered on the morning of 6 September, wearing civilian clothes, at a farm at Tournan-en-Brie, 32 km south-east of Paris. Court-martialled that same day, he pleaded not guilty, claiming that he had fallen out to answer a call of nature, only to find that his regiment had marched on before he had finished. Found guilty, Highgate was informed of his death sentence at 6.22 am on the 8th and, after three-quarters of an hour with a clergyman, was shot at 7.07 am. He was 19.

Three days later five other privates of the 1/Royal West Kent were also court-martialled. The offences, allegedly committed between 31 August and 10 September, included insubordination and the loss of equipment. One of them, Private Adams, was sentenced to six months' detention for causing the death of Sergeant Caleb Gilbey by a negligent discharge of his rifle. Gilbey's name is inscribed on the same panel of the memorial as Highgate's, for both their burial places are unknown.

Highgate was pardoned under the Armed Forces Act 2006. This has highlighted an anomaly, for even though his name is engraved on the monument at La Ferté-sous-Jouarre, he was not included on the village war memorial at Shoreham in Kent, his childhood home. In 2000 the parish council decided against adding his name, but the controversy was revived following his pardon, and remains un-resolved at the time of writing.

You will probably have spotted another anomaly. At the top of the monument is a stone sarcophagus, topped with a representation of a Tommy's steel helmet. In fact, the BEF wore flat caps at the start of the war, and helmets were introduced only in 1915–16.

Royal Engineers' memorial
Behind the monument is a little park. From it, walk along the river-bank path that passes under the bridge. As you emerge on the far side, you will see a stone pillar topped with a flaming grenade, an emblem of the Royal Engineers (RE). Together with its twin on the opposite bank, the pillar marks the location of the temporary bridge built across the Marne by two RE companies.

When the Germans finally withdrew from La Ferté-sous-Jouarre during the afternoon of the 9th, the RE were able to move down to the river and start assembling the necessary material. Covering troops were ferried across the river in boats, and towards 8.45 pm the RE began building the bridge. They did so 15 metres downstream of the destroyed permanent bridge, whose debris broke the force of the current. (The modern road bridge stands in the same place as its predecessor.) Work continued throughout the night and finished at 6.20 am on the 10th. It was an impressive achievement. The bridge was 61 metres long, not including the approaches that had to be cut

1/The Cameronians (Scottish Rifles) crossing the temporary bridge at La Ferté-sous-Jouarre, 10 September.

Royal Engineers' monument at the site of the temporary bridge.

3 metres deep through the banks to allow access. The total length including the approaches was 66 metres.

Since too few pontoons had been available to span such a wide river, the RE had been forced to find or improvise the remaining supports, along with most of the other items, including gunwales, planking and braces. Much of the wood had to be ripped out of buildings in the town, which helps explain why the work took all night. 'The actual last link was dramatic', recalled one of the RE officers, Lieutenant B.K. Young. Everything available had been put into the bridge, yet the two ends failed to meet. The situation was saved when Lieutenant R.G. Wright suddenly appeared in a boat that proved just sufficient to fill the gap, even if the safety margin for that final bay barely existed. Supporting the roadway was an odd assortment of four pontoons, two trestles, five piers made from barrels lashed together, and three barges or boats of various sizes.

Troops began to cross as soon as the bridge was finished, and the flow of men and vehicles continued throughout the day in an almost unbroken stream until 8.30 pm. 'We spent the whole of the 10th caring for that bridge,' wrote Lieutenant Young, 'while a ceaseless stream of traffic crossed without one single accident or hitch.' Work on dismantling the bridge began towards 4.30 am on the 11th, and was completed by 9.00. The two RE companies then marched off to the north, following the BEF's advance to the Aisne river.

Point 10: Perreuse *Château*
To complete your tour, retrieve your car and visit Perreuse *Château* cemetery, 4.5 km south-west of La Ferté-sous-Jouarre. (The name today is sometimes spelled Péreuse.) From the roundabout at the BEF Monument drive 200 metres westwards along the D603, across the Petit Morin river, and then turn left up the D402 (signposted for Jouarre). When you reach the top of the hill and come to the entrance to Jouarre, take the second right (signposted for Sept-Sorts and Signy-Signets). After 200 metres, at the roundabout, take the D114p and drive westwards for 2 km. Immediately after passing through Les Corbiers, turn left when you see the signposts for Perreuse *Château*. The road leads you past a pond and then uphill towards the *château*'s entrance. Before you reach the gates, turn off to the right and follow the white-on-green Commonwealth War Graves Commission (CWGC) sign for the cemetery. Ignore the next left-hand turning (signposted for Péreuse, it simply leads back to the *château* gates). Instead, continue straight ahead for another 400 metres,

along the northern side of the grounds. Turn left at the CWGC sign, and you will find the cemetery 250 metres down the track.

The BEF established a temporary hospital at Perreuse during the Battle of the Marne, and the *château* was used for the same purpose later in the war. Those of the wounded who died were buried in the grounds. The remains of other men were moved here from elsewhere. The cemetery contains both French and British dead from the two world wars, and a single US grave. You will notice that two of the graves from 1944 – those of Lieutenants Eric Cauchi and Armand Lansdell – have no regiment recorded on their headstones. They were, in fact, secret agents from the Special Operations Executive, which explains their vague designation as 'General List'. Here, too, lies Second Lieutenant Collingwood-Thompson, whose memorial we visited in La Ferté-sous-Jouarre. He died at the *château* towards 4.00 am on 10 September, as a result of his injuries, and is buried at Plot 1, Row D, Grave 46 (nearest the Cross of Sacrifice).

Also buried here is Lieutenant Colonel Louis St Gratien Le Marchant, the commander of the 1/East Lancashires (Plot 1, Row B, Grave 14). He had joined the regiment aged 19, and won the Distinguished Service Order while serving in South Africa in 1900–2. He was killed in La Ferté-sous-Jouarre on the morning of 9 September, when he was shot through the head by a sniper whilst examining

the German positions across the Marne from the window of a house on the south bank. (The date of death on his headstone is wrongly recorded as the 14th.) One of his men, Private Edward Roe, saw a body being carried past him on a stretcher covered by a blanket. The bearers told him it was that of a private, for they had been ordered to conceal the news of the lieutenant colonel's death, but they had to admit the truth since a boot and spur were visible beneath the blanket. Le Marchant was an outstanding leader, and had insisted on staying in command of his

Lieutenant Colonel Le Marchant.

battalion despite being lamed at the Battle of Le Cateau on 26 August. On the morning of his death he was personally seeking out the best firing positions, and checking that they were not too exposed for his men. Officers of Le Marchant's quality formed the backbone of the BEF of 1914. Their loss was sorely felt in the months that followed, as the British army began expanding from a small, professional force to a colossal military machine of 4 million men, while also trying to adapt to ongoing changes in the very nature of warfare.

Tour 6

FOCH'S VICTORY

Most of this book concentrates on the experiences of the ordinary soldiers, but this particular tour focuses on one of the French army commanders struggling to control a vast, sprawling battle with limited means of communication. It is a study of the impact of *Général de division* Ferdinand Foch, the larger-than-life personality who commanded the *9e armée*. The tour will visit his headquarters and command posts, consider the impact of his decisions, and debate the merits of this pivotal, but controversial, figure.

'What's the problem?'

Surprisingly, Foch had never once seen action before 1914. His service during the previous war against Germany in 1870–1 had been limited to garrison duties, and he lacked any colonial postings. Most of his career had been spent in staff appointments, or else at the *Ecole de guerre* (first as an instructor, and later as the commandant).

Foch studied his profession deeply, especially the campaigns of Napoleon and those of Moltke the Elder. He realized that a commander had little time to think while a battle was actually in progress, and so had to rely on instinct. Studying the art of war in peacetime helped form the instinctive judgement needed to take good, timely decisions. In 1903 and 1904 Foch published two volumes of his lectures – *Des principes de la guerre*, and *De la conduite de la guerre*. His tactical ideas have been criticized by historians, but often unjustly, for he was not, in fact, blind to the importance of firepower – in *Des principes*, he recognized that massed artillery fire was needed to prepare an attack. He did emphasize the offensive, but made the obvious point that a purely defensive attitude could not destroy the enemy. Only an offensive could produce results. 'Every defensive battle must therefore end with an offensive action,

Foch.

a riposte, a victorious counter-attack, or there is no result.' Foch knew that it was difficult for a commander to communicate with his units at the forward edge of a battle while it was under way, and so the most effective means he had of influencing the outcome was to inculcate an aggressive spirit in his subordinates, in the knowledge that this attitude would percolate down through the ranks.

Foch was no mere professor – not one of those brittle, intellectual commanders who prove unequal to the strain of high command in wartime. Instead, he was a man of action. Despite being 62 at the time of the Marne, he was fit and active, and during the war made a point of taking a walk almost every day. He communicated energy and decisiveness. Just 5 foot 6 inches in height, he had short legs, but a disproportionately large head, enhanced by a jutting jaw and large moustache. His piercing eyes darted around, taking in everything at a glance, and he reinforced his quick, direct and sometimes abrupt speech with vigorous gestures, to a degree unusual even for the French.

'The general is a *man*' wrote his chief of staff, *Lieutenant-colonel* Maxime Weygand, 'one of the exceptional men to appear in these times. Everyone recognises his ability. He gives us a great example of leadership.' Foch immediately gripped whatever situation confronted him. Typically, his first question was: *De quoi s'agit-il?* – 'What's the problem?' It was designed to get instantly to the heart of the matter. In finding a solution, Foch used his commonsense, and ensured he knew how his superiors' minds worked, so he could obey the spirit of his orders in pursuit of their overall intention.

Once Foch had reached a decision, he rarely changed his mind. He looked forward, without becoming bogged down in difficulties or

past mistakes. His studies had convinced him of the overriding importance of morale and leadership. Victory depended not on a fierce, inflexible adhesion to a particular doctrine, but on a triumph of the spirit. He was a man of human warmth, blessed with a happy marriage and sustained by a staunch, religious faith – he had been educated partly at a Jesuit college. He was driven, too, by bitter memories of France's defeat in 1870–1, when his best friend from the Jesuit college had been killed in action.

Weygand.

In an age of industrialized warfare Foch knew that the human touch was more vital than ever, and that the impersonal command methods of the German General Staff were no substitute for the moral courage, personal grip and buoyant optimism of a true leader.

WHAT HAPPENED

In the opening month of the war Foch proved himself a capable and aggressive corps commander, and was picked by Joffre to command a newly created army – the *9e armée* – to fill a gap that had emerged in the centre of the retreating Allied line. When the retreat came to an end on 5 September, Foch prepared to play a pivotal role in the counter-offensive. From the very start of the Battle of the Marne he had a dual mission. In the west he had to cover the right flank of the advancing *5e armée* with attacks of his own. Yet in the east he needed to hold an over-extended front against increasing German pressure, and maintain contact with the neighbouring *4e armée*.

Since Foch's centre was covered by the St-Gond marshes, the heaviest fighting occurred on either wing. The terrain here was starkly different. On the Brie plateau in the west it was similar to the intricate countryside that the BEF had to cross: hills, rivers and patches of woodland. In the east, in contrast, lay a vast, barren and undulating plain. Here and there it was covered with pine woods, but in general it offered few advantages for a defender. The most pronounced feature on this wing was *Mont Août*, an isolated hill behind the French lines that dominated the surrounding countryside.

The *9e armée* was a composite force, hurriedly cobbled together and fully activated as an army just a couple of days before the start of Joffre's offensive. Particularly troubling was the existence of an almost 20-km gap between Foch's right flank and the *4e armée*, which he could merely mask with a cavalry division. Fortunately, the German *3. Armee* opposite Foch was pulled in either direction by demands for support from its neighbours: it was actually torn in two, and had a gap of its own in the middle, corresponding with that on Foch's right.

The pressure on Foch intensified with every passing day. At first, on 6 and 7 September, the situation was one of stalemate, with both

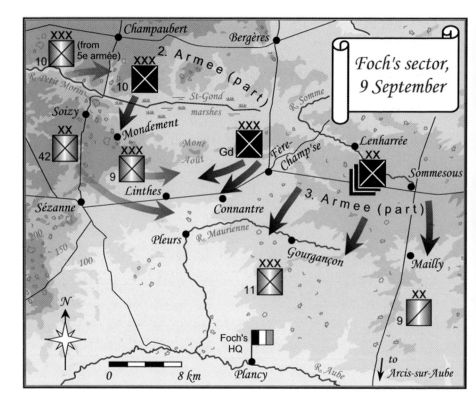

Champaubert

Bergères

XXX (from 5e armée)

10

XXX

10

2. Armee (part)

St-Gond marshes

R. Somme

Foch's sector, 9 September

Soizy

R. Petit Morin

Mondement

Mont Août

Gd

XXX

Fère-Champ'se

Lenharrée

XX

Sommesous

XX

42

XXX

9

Linthes

3. Armee (part)

Connantre

Sézanne

200

150

100

Pleurs

R. Maurienne

Gourgançon

Mailly

XXX

11

XX

9

N

Foch's HQ

0   8 km   Plancy

R. Aube

to Arcis-sur-Aube

sides making only modest and temporary gains. But then, early on the morning of the 8th, three German infantry divisions suddenly fell on Foch's right wing. The attack came as a surprise, for it dispensed with a preliminary artillery bombardment and was deliberately launched under the cover of darkness to avoid the devastating fire from the French 75mm guns. Some of Foch's units fought back hard, inflicting heavy casualties and breaking the German momentum, but the wing as a whole collapsed under the shock, and stumbled back 8 km, from the Somme stream to the vicinity of the Maurienne, losing even the town of Fère-Champenoise. Foch ordered a counter-attack, but it regained only a limited amount of ground, and the Germans were halted largely by their own confusion and tiredness – partly as they had attacked in the dark and at so early an hour – and by a breakdown in the coordination of their divisions.

Bold solution

Foch knew that his battered eastern wing would be overwhelmed the next day unless he took decisive action, yet he had no more troops in reserve. His solution was bold and imaginative. Appealing for help from the neighbouring *5e armée*, he secured the loan of an army corps, which in turn enabled him on the 9th to pull the *42e division* – one of his best formations – out of the line on his western wing, and move it behind his army, off the Brie plateau and down into the open plain to restore the situation in the east. Yet the difficulties – the friction that slows any enterprise – delayed the execution of this plan so long that the *42e division* nearly failed to arrive. After being relieved five hours later than expected, it had to march some 15 km in intense heat to the vicinity of Linthes, where it finally appeared towards 4.00 pm.

Meanwhile, the knowledge that the *42e division* was on its way helped hold the *9e armée* together in the face of a renewed German offensive. The mere sight of the division's arrival boosted morale. 'Descending from the heights of Allemant', wrote *Lieutenant-colonel* Weygand, 'in faultless order, without visible fatigue after the three days of bloody fighting ... such was the appearance of this fine unit led by its "backbone", *Général* Grossetti.'

The German advance finally ground to a halt that afternoon, when the order came to retreat in order to extricate the armies nearer Paris from their increasingly dangerous situation. Even so, it was nearly 6.00 pm by the time that Foch's staff had organized a general counter-attack, and less than an hour of daylight remained. The *9e armée* ended up making only a few disjointed advances that evening, rather than a powerful onslaught all along the line. The *42e division*, for example, rolled forward from the area south-west of Linthes, but was halted by the onset of dusk after covering barely 3 km, up to the D205 (the road linking Linthes and Pleurs). Other units did not get under way until the next morning, by which time they were simply pursuing an already-retreating foe – yet it must be remembered that the pursuit would have been even slower to start if Foch had not insisted on a counter-offensive.

It was during the Battle of the Marne that Foch is supposed to have made a now-famous remark. 'My centre is giving way, my right is falling back,' he announced. 'Situation excellent. I attack.' In

French troops resist the German advance. Some trenches were dug during the battle, but, as here, they were generally shallow and hastily made.

fact, this is one of the great myths of the battle, although the words do reflect his undaunted spirit and the critical nature of his position. A purely passive defence would have been fatal, whereas a more active approach, with its flexible combination of both defence and attack, did at least stop hard-pressed subordinates from looking to the rear, and reduced the risk of their formations falling apart during a demoralizing retreat. Foch had the breadth of vision to realize that the fierceness of the German onslaughts on him reflected the fact that the battle was going badly for them elsewhere. He later said that his merit at the Marne had been to see the situation clearly. His biggest single decision was to transfer the *42e division* to the eastern wing, but it was the general spirit he infused into his army that was the most remarkable aspect of his performance. He knew that battles were won and lost in the minds of the troops and their commanders. 'A battle won is a battle in which you will not admit yourself to be beaten,' he had written in *Des principes*. By demanding counter-attacks from exhausted and half-defeated formations – by imposing on them his own, unshakeable faith in victory – he enabled his army to hold on until the tide turned. At the Marne he proved the correctness of Joffre's decision to give him an army command, and took the first great leap in the ascent that would carry him in 1918 to supreme command on the Western Front.

WHAT TO SEE

After considering the battle from Foch's perspective, we will visit some key locations on his eastern wing where the actual fighting took place. The tour starts at Plancy-l'Abbaye, where Foch had his headquarters, some 20 km south of the combat zone. To reach it from the city of Troyes, head north along the D677 (formerly designated the N77) in the direction of Châlons-en-Champagne. After passing through Arcis-sur-Aube, turn left on to the D56 and follow it westwards to Plancy.

Point 1: Plancy-l'Abbaye

Foch arrived at Plancy on 5 September, the eve of the battle. The town was a particularly fitting location for his headquarters, since one of his heroes, Napoleon, had stayed at the local *château* during the 1814 campaign. Foch established his office in the house of *père* Louis Brisson, a local clergyman who until his death in 1908 had devoted himself to helping and educating the poor. The house is near the church, at 1 *bis*, *rue du père Brisson*. The residents (the *Congrégation des Sœurs Oblates de St François de Sales*) occasionally hold open-days when it is possible to see the room that Foch used. Inside, you will find Foch's portrait, along with a handwritten note expressing gratitude for the hospitality shown to him.

Although this was where Foch had his office, he slept at another nearby house. Each morning he would briefly enter the church, and then go forward to a command post at Pleurs, 15 km to the northwest, from where he could control the battle more closely. He later claimed that whenever he left Plancy, the family on whom he was billeted would pack so as to be ready to flee at a moment's notice. Reassured by his return in the evening, they would unpack again, only to repeat the process the next day.

Plancy: the house of **père** *Brisson.*

On 9 September Foch had to remain at Plancy, for that final day of the battle brought the Germans to within 4 km of Pleurs. He felt unable to visit his corps commanders in the field, since after less than a fortnight in command he lacked a fully functional staff to handle matters in his absence. Tied to his headquarters, he relied heavily on the telephone, and periodically sent orders and bulletins, which kept his subordinates informed of the wider situation. Towards noon he issued a characteristically upbeat appeal to boost the morale of his army. Explaining that the Germans were utterly exhausted, he called on his men to make a final effort. 'The disorder prevailing among the German troops is the sign of impending victory,' he promised. 'But everyone must be convinced that success will go to the side that endures the longer.' Foch also made systematic use of liaison officers as his eyes and ears on the battlefield. In particular, he

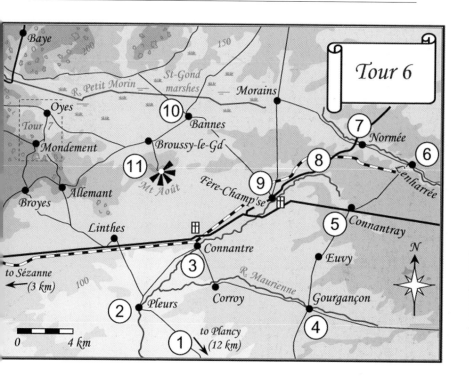

sent his chief of staff, Weygand, to coordinate the counter-offensive he had ordered for that afternoon. It proved an effective way of keeping a grip on the battle, despite its scale and his inability to leave Plancy.

Before you leave Plancy, visit the *mairie* at 13, *rue Pierre Labonde*. A small plaque next to the door records Foch's stay at the town.

Point 2: Pleurs

Now head out of Plancy along the D7, heading north. Pass through Champfleury, Salon, Faux-Fresnay and Courcelles, and park in the centre of Pleurs. Foch's command post was at the *mairie* (6, *rue de la Libération*), where you will find a plaque on the wall. He came here on 6, 7 and 8 September. Until the German breakthrough on the morning of the 8th, Pleurs lay 16–20 km south-west of the front line, but by the 9th it had become too exposed for Foch to return.

Foch's command post: the **mairie** *at Pleurs.*

Point 3: Connantre

Our next stop is Connantre, which lies 4 km to the north-east along the D305a. From the *mairie* of Pleurs, head 25 metres north-westwards along the *rue de la Libération* and you will see the turning for Connantre on your right.

Connantre fell to the German *Gardekorps* in the afternoon of 9 September. Its proximity to Pleurs is a reminder of just how far Foch's army was forced back before the tide turned. But the Germans paid a heavy price for their gains. On the northern side of Connantre a military cemetery contains the remains of more than 8,900 of their soldiers, three-quarters of the number of dead at Tyne Cot in Belgium, which is the largest Commonwealth war graves cemetery in the world.

To reach the cemetery, drive straight through the centre of Connantre; turn left when you come to the *chaussée du Pont de pierre*, and follow it out of town. You will see signs for the *Deutscher Soldatenfriedhof*. Pass under the road bridge, and then turn left over the level-crossing. Turn left again on the other side of the railway, and head west for 500 metres until you come to an un-signposted track leading off to a clump of trees on the right. The cemetery is completely hidden amid these trees. Since this is a German cemetery, in a country invaded by the Germans, it is deliberately unobtrusive, and occupies a remarkably small area considering the number of men buried here – it is less than a quarter of the extent of Tyne Cot.

More than nine-tenths of the dead lie in mass graves. Among those buried separately is *Leutnant* Werner, *Graf* von Moltke (Grave 298). He was not an immediate relative of the Chief of the General Staff, but belonged to the extended Moltke family. The Moltkes had been landowners in Mecklenburg, on the Baltic coast, for an almost unbroken stretch of more than five centuries, which explains why Werner belonged to the (*Grossherzoglich Mecklenburgisches*) *Grenadier-Regiment Nr 89*. Four of the Moltkes had served in the regiment's antecedent units. One, a battalion commander, had died during Napoleon's retreat from Russia in 1812, when the Mecklenburgers had been part of the *Grande armée*. Werner fell at the start of the Battle of the Marne, on 6 September, when his regiment lost heavily against the French *5e armée* near the *Château d'Esternay*, 24 km west of Connantre. His remains were moved here after the end of the war, as part of the policy of collecting the fallen German soldiers into a limited number of cemeteries.

Return to the centre of Connantre, but watch out for one-way signs as you re-enter the town – you will need to take a slightly different route from the one you used on the way out. Park near the church and visit the local civilian cemetery (a 200-metre walk to the north-west along the *rue des Ecoles*). Here, beneath the wall on the left shortly after you enter, is a memorial to *Caporal* Louis Bénard of the *290e régiment*. He was killed on the morning of 9 September when his company advanced through a wood east of Connantre and was suddenly fired on by German infantry at close range. The stone initially marked the place where he fell, but was later transferred to this cemetery.

Point 4: Gourgançon

Leave Connantre by taking the D305 at the roundabout in front of the church. The road leads you to Corroy, 2.5 km to the southeast. When you reach the T-junction inside Corroy, turn left and follow the signposts for Gourgançon. You are now driving alongside the Maurienne stream on your left, which marked the limit of the German advance on 9 September. The battered units of Foch's *11e corps* held the higher ground about 1 km on your right. The terrain differs from how it looked at the time of the battle, for the widescale use of fertiliser and farm machinery has transformed this previously barren and impoverished region – *Champagne pouilleuse* – into productive farmland. In 1914 the open countryside through which you are passing was generally used for grazing livestock, and was partly covered with pine woods rather than with the wind

Gourgançon. The village marked the limit of German progress.

Ruined houses at Gourgançon after the battle.

turbines of today. The village of Gourgançon was occupied in the afternoon of the 9th by elements of the Saxon 24. *Reserve-Infanterie-Division*. It was left in ruins, having been shelled and set ablaze, although its church escaped serious damage.

Point 5: Connantray

Until Foch's right wing was thrust back on the morning of the 8th, it had held a position along the Somme, some 8–10 km north of Gourgançon. We shall now examine one sector of that initial front line, at Lenharrée and Normée, with a preliminary stop at Connantray. At Gourgançon church turn left on to the D43, and follow it to Euvy. On reaching the crossroads in the centre of Euvy, turn right down the *rue Haute*. (The turning is unsignposted, but you will see the church and the *mairie* on the opposite side of the D43 at this point.) Continue along the *rue Haute*, past the water-tower, and on to Connantray.

When you come to the 'Stop' sign at Connantray, turn right on to the N4. After just 125 metres, take the first left, down the *rue de l'Eglise*.

Continue to the church and then park your car. Go up the flight of steps into the churchyard, and walk round to visit the military plot on the far side of the church. Five of the fifteen French soldiers buried here are from the *114e régiment*, all of whom died on 8 September. That morning the regiment was in the second line, 2 km north of Connantray, as part of the *18e division*, when the French front broke under the impact of the German onslaught. Amidst the confusion, the 2nd Battalion was mistakenly shelled by French guns, and its commander, *Capitaine* Jean-Marie Cazalas, who had already been wounded by German artillery fire, was killed. With him died *Médecin auxiliaire* Henri Michel, who, as the regimental war diary records, was caring for Cazalas 'with a devotion beyond all praise'. *Capitaine* Eugène Aimé was sent back to the French batteries to stop the friendly fire, but was later found dead on the road west of Connantray, having been killed during the return trip. The commander of the 3rd Battalion, *Capitaine* Paul Bosquet de Malabry, also fell, as did one of his company commanders, *Capitaine* Henri Bréart de Boisanger, a Breton poet and novelist. Note the inscription on Boisanger's tomb – an extract from a letter he wrote to his wife two days before he fell. 'The moment has come for thinking only of God and of France', he informed her. 'I am firing up my spirit, and that of my men, at the prospect of laying down our lives.'

From Connantray church drive back down the *rue de l'Eglise* for 50 metres before turning left down the *ruelle du Gué*. At the end of this winding street turn left again (on to the *route de Lenharrée*, although you will not see it named at this point). Continue north-eastwards along this road for 5 km to the village of Lenharrée.

Point 6: Lenharrée
As you drive towards Lenharrée, note how sparsely populated the plain is. The few villages tend to be concentrated along the streams, and this is what made the Somme an obvious line of defence: although fordable, it had a string of villages that could be turned into strongholds.

Park in the centre of Lenharrée, and then climb the *rue vallée de la Somme* as it bends to the right, up the slopes north of the stream. At the *mairie* turn left up the *ruelle de l'Eglise* to reach the church. Note how it is perched right on the edge of the plateau above the Somme valley, making it the main bastion in the village.

Just inside the churchyard, examine the local war memorial. On the sides are engraved the names of four civilians who died on 7 September, two of whom are buried close by – 66-year-old Ernest Felix, and Stephanie Hemart, who was 82. Go round to the western side of the church, and you will see a stone column that commemorates the French soldiers who defended the village, and in particular the 540 of them who died. Nineteen of these fallen men are named. Most are from the *19e régiment* (although *Sous-lieutenant*

Monument des Bretons, *at Lenharrée.*

Eugène Brodhag is wrongly listed: he actually belonged to the *225e régiment*, part of the *60e division de réserve*). The column is known as the *Monument des Bretons*, for the *19e*, along with the rest of the *22e division*, came from Brittany. To the left of the monument are the graves of three of the French soldiers, including *Soldat* Lucien Penther of the *19e*, who was killed by a shell burst on 7 September, and *Capitaine* Henri de Saint-Bon of the *225e*, whose wife was buried with him when she died more than forty years later.

The *19e régiment* held Lenharrée throughout 6 and 7 September, but was then relieved. On the 8th the village was defended by two companies of the *225e*, and a battalion each from the *62e* and *116e régiments*. These were the units that had to face the German onslaught that morning by elements of the *Garde-Grenadier-Regiment Nr 4* and of the Saxon *32. Infanterie-Division*. The attack started at 3.00 am. The Germans approached through the woods, which at the time of the battle extended up to 2 km from the Somme. *Unteroffizier* Walter Frenzel, of *Infanterie-Regiment Nr 103*, recalled how he stumbled forwards, still half-asleep. 'Then at last the wood thinned out, and we emerged on to open ground, and were jolted from our dreams by a sudden glow. Beyond the high ground, a village [Lenharrée] was burning, and the light gleamed high into the sky. On the rising ground stood thick skirmish lines and assault columns. Flags fluttered in the gentle, morning breeze, but otherwise it was completely calm and quiet.'

Suddenly an order was passed from man to man: 'Unload rifles!', followed by 'Fix bayonets!'. Commanders did not want their units to become bogged down in a firefight, for that would destroy the momentum of the attack. Frenzel, now fully alert, peered ahead into the darkness. The assault began and the first shells whistled over-head. The Saxons found some French soldiers asleep in trenches, and clubbed them with rifle-butts, before continuing the advance. In the distance Frenzel could hear indistinct shouting, roars of 'hurrah!', and then the sound of the Saxons singing *Die Wacht am Rhein*. 'We stormed forwards in a blind frenzy', he wrote, 'and suddenly found ourselves – a little band of 100 men – in the garden of a farmhouse, illuminated by the pale, flickering light of the flames.' They scaled a wall and pushed on into Lenharrée. Amid the hand-to-hand fighting, Frenzel heard insane laughter and men screaming as they died.

The fighting at Lenharrée.

Lenharrée church today.

The defenders forced the Germans to take the village house by house. When *Capitaine* de Saint-Bon was mortally wounded, he forbade his men to help him. 'Leave me be,' he called. 'Don't get yourselves killed trying to rescue me.' It was almost 5.00 am before Lenharrée finally fell. The toughest fight raged at the church, where the French held on tenaciously, supported by several machine-guns. 'The first assault failed bloodily,' wrote a Saxon platoon commander. 'In the second, the church, too, was taken. As we advanced further through the village, we were pelted by a devastating fire from windows and skylights. Many houses had to be set on fire, as all the entrances were barricaded. The French had nestled even in the poplar trees in order to shoot at us.'

Leave the church, and follow the German advance down the slope to the Somme. At the time of the battle the stream was about 2 metres wide and 1.5 metres deep. The heat from the blazing buildings had made the atmosphere unbearable in the narrow streets. *Unteroffizier* Frenzel recalled how his comrades scooped up some of the water in their hands as they waded across the Somme, in order to quench their thirst. He himself was wounded soon afterwards.

The German onslaught was losing momentum. Already more than two hours had passed since the start of the attack. Even after the Germans had seized Lenharrée and breached the line of the Somme, they encountered another defence line on the high ground less than 1 km to the south, where the French were holding a railway embankment that ran parallel to the stream. You can easily identify this position today: it is the line of trees and bushes at the point where the Connantray road passes the massive silos. (The railway tracks have now been partly dismantled.) One of the defenders of this line was *Sergent* Charles Penther of the *19e régiment* – the brother of Lucien, whose grave we visited in the churchyard. It was barely daylight but he could make out the plain in front. 'What was this?' he wondered. 'It was a confused horde – the plain swarmed with troops who were impossible to identify. Some officers near me thought they recognized the Germans, and ordered us to shoot. Others shouted that it was a mistake, and tried to stop the firing, for they believed they had spotted French uniforms. In reality, as we discovered later, both were right, but their contradictory orders threw us into consternation.'

Some time later Penther noticed that the stones of the embankment were splintering under the impact of bullets fired from behind him. German detachments had broken through further west, and were now sweeping the rear of the railway line with rifle and machine-gun fire. Penther's officers debated what to do: make a bayonet charge, or fall back towards the woods across 500 metres of open plain. After preparing to charge, they changed their minds and abandoned their positions. Immediately the Germans climbed the embankment and fired into the backs of the fleeing men. 'It was a real massacre', Penther wrote. He himself had no idea how he survived, for he was one of the last to leave and yet he escaped with just a bullet in the wrist.

Fortunately for Penther, the Germans had also lost heavily, partly because too many of their units had become drawn into a constricted area in order to overcome the resistance at Lenharrée. They were now tired, disorganized and unable to maintain the tempo of their advance. Frenzel's *Infanterie-Regiment Nr 103*, for example, had to halt and collect its scattered elements near the railway line. It saw no further fighting that day and bivouacked for the night at Connantray, barely 4 km to the south-west. It was left with just one staff officer, one *Hauptmann*, and a handful of *Leutnants*.

Point 7: Normée

Retrieve your car and head out of Lenharrée along the D18, following the Somme valley to the neighbouring village of Normée, 4 km to the north-west. Much of Normée was burned down during the battle. Inside the church you will find a plaque commemorating the *42e brigade*, from the Vendée in western France, which held this sector. The brigade lost Normée on 6 September, but then held the line of the railway, 1 km further south. On the 8th it broke under the German onslaught after suddenly coming under fire from the rear. Its commander, *Colonel* Jean-Alfred Lamey, was killed near the level-crossing that used to exist where the railway crossed the D5.

If you have time, you can visit a monument to one of Lamey's men, *Maréchal-des-logis* Antoine Cardin. It lies at the end of a farm track, so you should leave your car at Normée and go on foot. The total distance there and back is 3.5 km. At the eastern entrance to Normée turn right up the minor road that passes a silo. Continue

DIEU
HONNEUR - PATRIE
ICI, DE NORMÉE A LENHARRÉE
LES 5, 6, 7, 8 SEPTEMBRE - 1914
SOUS LE COMMANDEMENT DU COLONEL LAMEY
ET A SON EXEMPLE
SA 42ᴱ BRIGADE DE VENDÉE
137ᴱ RI - 93ᴱ RI - 51ᴱ R.A. (1ᴱᴿ ET 3ᴹᴱ GR)
SELON SA MISSION
TINT JUSQU'A LA MORT
ET BRISA L'ATTAQUE ENNEMIE.

Normée: the plaque inside the church.

Cardin monument.

straight ahead to the south-west for 1 km – the road soon becomes a track – heading for the line of bushes on the horizon. (Ignore both the right-hand turning shortly after the silo and the left-hand turning halfway to the bushes.) Just before the track passes through a gap in the line of bushes, turn left, so you end up walking south-eastwards, keeping the bushes immediately on your right. You will come to the monument after another 750 metres. The bushes mark the former course of the railway line, and it was here that Cardin fell on 8 September. He belonged to the *3e dragons*, but was with the *137e régiment* when he died. His remains were later reburied at his home town in the Vendée.

Point 8: Zehrfuss monument
From Normée, drive south-westwards along the D5 to Fère-Champenoise. After 3 km, at the left-hand edge of the road, stands a small memorial to *Capitaine* Henri Zehrfuss. (You will find a lay-by at this point, where you can park briefly.) Zehrfuss was serving as a staff officer with the *18e division*. The division was deployed in support of the *11e corps*, which was holding the front line along the Somme stream, but was placed too close behind it and without establishing proper liaison. When the Germans attacked on the morning of the 8th, much of the *18e division* became swept up in the débâcle. From his headquarters at Fère-Champenoise, the divisional commander sent Zehrfuss towards Normée to find out what was happening in that sector, but Zehrfuss was killed when his car ran into the German advance. He left behind a two-year-old son, Bernard, who later became one of France's leading architects.

Interestingly, a German soldier has described shooting up a French car 1.5 km further down the road, and was possibly referring to the same incident. He was *Füsilier* Amrhein of the *Garde-Grenadier-Regiment Nr 1*. He wrote:

An enemy motorcar, which had already been shot at from further on our left, came racing along the road towards Fère-Champenoise. We, too, opened fire, and it suddenly veered off the road and into the field, coming to a standstill close to the brook. *Gefreiter* Reimann and I dashed towards it, but received a hail of fire, so we took up position in the road ditch, and shot at the occupants. Their fire soon fell silent, and then we went over. The driver was wounded. An officer sitting inside the car had been killed by several shots to his head – he appeared, from his gold-embroidered képi, to be a general. Beside him was another officer, likewise dead, who had been hit in the head and chest. Both of them had valuable maps and papers, which we took and afterwards handed over to the staff of the *3. Garde-Infanterie-Brigade*.

Capitaine *Zehrfuss.*

Monument to Zehrfuss.

Point 9: Fère-Champenoise

Drive the rest of the way to Fère-Champenoise. As you approach the town, you come to a roundabout, where the D9 arrives from the right. Continue straight ahead, along the D5 (signposted for Paris, Provins, and Fère-Champenoise), but then, 100 metres beyond the roundabout, turn off to the right (signposted for Fère-Champenoise). This road will lead you into the town centre, where you can park and have a look around.

Fère-Champenoise was important because it was the only sizeable town in Foch's sector. It was also the central road hub: it straddles both the N4 to Paris in the west, and the D9, which runs past the eastern tip of the St-Gond marshes. The German *Gardekorps* captured the town in the afternoon of 8 September, after Foch's right wing had collapsed under the onslaught launched early that morning. A *Leutnant* of the *Garde-Grenadier-Regiment Nr 1* was among those who entered Fère-Champenoise. 'We were all exhausted', he wrote, 'for it was very hot, and the reaction to the morning's excitement now set in.' He sat on a stool at the corner of the main square, and feasted on bread and marmalade, washed down with champagne and red wine. Masses of troops had arrived, and were looking for food. The divisional staff drove up. 'Gradually, we found out the casualties. The joy of victory disappeared, and gave way to a deadly serious-ness.' Then the commander of the *Gardekorps*, *General der Infanterie* Karl, *Freiherr* von Plettenberg, appeared. 'He stopped nearby, and waved to us. His son was an orderly officer in the divisional staff, and leaped on to the running-board of the car to give his father a kiss. The old man was deeply affected by this battle.'

Yet the fighting was far from over, as was made clear when two shrapnel shells suddenly exploded, leaving smoke-clouds hanging in the sky. 'Do the French never go away?' the *Leutnant* wondered. 'It appears not.' Indeed, the tide of battle turned the next day, and the French were back in Fère-Champenoise early on 10 September. Foch himself reached the town towards noon, and found that it had been completely pillaged. 'I never saw such a sight', he later recalled. 'The streets were so bristling with shards of broken bottles that we were literally unable to go forward, whether by motorcar, horse, or foot. Ah, *messieurs les Boches* had had a wild time the day before – such a wild time that hundreds of them were still sleeping off their wine in the cellars. I saw some of them on the roofs, running like cats, and being shot at in volleys.'

Foch wanted to push on at once to the north of Fère-Champenoise, but was told that the road was too exposed to artillery fire for him to do so. He instead went to the railway station, 1 km north-west of the town along the D43, which was the command post of his *9e corps*.

Fère-Champenoise: the railway station after the battle.

The station today.

Here, he tried to increase the tempo of the pursuit. 'The roof was burning above us as we studied our maps', Foch recalled. 'Wooden beams cracked. We paid no attention. ... Hard work. At the end of the day, I could do no more.' The station still exists, but the line no longer carries passengers.

Foch established his headquarters in the *mairie* in the central square of the town (now the *place Georges Clémenceau*). It stank. A rotting horse lay beside the entrance steps, and wounded men cluttered the interior. There was no electricity, since the cables had been cut, and so candles were stuck into the necks of bottles. Foch was so tired that it made little difference. 'I slept like a log that night', he said. 'And yet this was at the *mairie* of Fère, full of comings and goings, amid an infernal noise, on an old mattress that had been laid out for Weygand and myself in a room that echoed like a bell.' In the early hours he was awoken to be informed that he had been made a *grand-officier* of the *Légion d'honneur*. 'Fine! Fine!'

The **mairie** *at Fère-Champenoise.*

he replied, and went back to sleep. Later, he was roused again, this time to be told that Joffre's headquarters had sent him some cigars and blankets. These were worth being awoken for, as the nights were cold. On the south-eastern side of Fère-Champenoise is a large French military cemetery. Created in 1920, it contains the remains of over 5,800 men who died in the surrounding area. Among them are some of the defenders of Lenharrée, including *Capitaine* Louis Deschard of the *19e régiment* (grave 1425), and *Sous-lieutenant* Eugène Brodhag of the *225e* (grave 181). For Foch himself the joy of victory was quickly followed by heartbreak, for within days he learned that his son-in-law had been killed three weeks earlier, and that his son was missing. His reaction was characteristically robust. Asking for some time alone, he spent half an hour in his office and then summoned his staff officers. 'Now let us get on with our work', he told them.

Point 10: Bannes

Having visited Foch's eastern wing, we shall end the tour by seeing the centre of his position, on the southern side of the St-Gond marshes. From Fère-Champenoise drive 8 km north-westwards along the D43 to Bannes. The marshes lie to the north of the village, and helped protect the central part of Foch's sector. Even though many parts have since been drained, they remain a formidable obstacle because of their dense tangle of vegetation. In 1914 the area was a mass of reeds, up to 3 km wide, intersected by rows of poplar trees along the five minor roads that crossed the marshes from north to south. In the dry season a person could walk over most of the marshes, except for some dangerous spots, but horses, vehicles and military units that wanted to preserve their cohesion were restricted to the roads, and these became obvious targets for artillery fire.

One of the myths about the battle was that the Prussian *Gardekorps* drowned during its attacks across these marshes. This was no more than propaganda, reminiscent of the exaggerated tales of Napoleon's victory at Austerlitz in 1805, when an entire wing of the Austro-Russian army was supposedly swallowed up in some ice-encrusted lakes. Claiming that the élite *Garde* had been destroyed was an obvious way of countering any notions that might exist of German invincibility.

If you wish to explore the marshes, visit the nature reserve at Reuves, 8 km west of Bannes. (Follow the signposts for the *marais de Reuves*. The final turning is easy to miss, but lies 100 metres beyond the northern exit of Reuves, on the eastern side of the road.)

Point 11: *Mont Août*

Our final stop, the hill of *Mont Août*, offers spectacular views across much of Foch's sector, and is a good point from which to visualize his situation as a whole. From Bannes drive 3.5 km south-westwards along the D39 to Broussy-le-Grand. Then turn left along the *rue des Buchettes*, which leads southwards to the summit of *Mont Août*. It is easy to overshoot the turning, as it lacks a signpost, although the streetname is visible. You will find it opposite a red fire-hydrant, shortly after you enter Broussy.

The importance of *Mont Août* is obvious, for the hill towers some 60–100 metres above the surrounding plain. It is an isolated fragment of the Brie plateau, which ends abruptly in the escarpment you can see 5 km to the west near Allemant. As we have noted earlier, the plain below lacks good viewpoints, and that was why *Mont Août* was so vital: it was a superb observation point for the French. More recently the summit hosted a NATO communications base, which has now closed. The road to the summit is tarmacked, but from there you will need to walk along sometimes muddy paths for views to the south and east.

The sight of *Mont Août* mesmerized the attacking German soldiers, such as *Vizewachtmeister* Schulz of the *Garde-Feldartillerie-Regiment Nr 1*. On the morning of 9 September he was facing the hill from a position 6 km to the east. 'For three days we had been constantly fighting the enemy', he wrote. 'Out of the morning mist, this hill rose once more before us.... Its round, tree-covered top reared threateningly over the entire region, and held everyone's attention.' Schulz was uncomfortably aware that French artillery observers were sitting up on the hill, watching the German movements.

By 10.00 am on the 9th the French had been driven right back to *Mont Août*, which became a bastion on a front line that now ran south-eastwards to Nozet farm and the village of Connantre. The hill was pounded by heavy-calibre shells as the Germans tried to soften up the defence. A battalion of the *1. Garde-Regiment zu Fuß*

Mont Août, *seen from the German cemetery at Connantre.*

advanced almost to the eastern foot of the hill, but had orders to wait there, under the cover of a now-vanished wood, until the French had been crushed by the artillery fire.

Early in the afternoon the defenders of *Mont Août* retreated after their flank was exposed by units further south giving way. When German patrols ventured up to the top of the hill, they found it deserted, but the main body of their battalion stayed below, and so *Mont Août* was practically unoccupied by either side for the rest of the day.

The next tour in this book examines the dramatic struggle for the *Château de Mondement*, a key stronghold on Foch's western wing. To reach the village of Oyes, where the tour starts, drive back to Broussy-le-Grand, and then turn left on to the D39. After 2 km turn right on to the D44, which leads you through Broussy-le-Petit and Reuves, and arrives at Oyes.

Tour 7

THE FIGHT FOR MONDEMENT

This final tour lies within the sector of the French *9e armée* under *Général de division* Ferdinand Foch. In Tour 6 we saw how Foch narrowly contained the German advance against his eastern wing on 9 September, but an equally fierce action raged that same day towards the western end of his line, at the *Château de Mondement*. It was one of the most dramatic and famous episodes of the entire battle.

WHAT HAPPENED

Early on the morning of the 9th a Hanoverian unit, *Infanterie-Regiment Nr 164*, managed to seize the fortress-like *château* on top of the escarpment above the St-Gond marshes. For the French this was a potentially fatal disaster. If the Germans managed to reinforce and expand their foothold at Mondement, they could conquer the rest of the high ground near Broyes and Allemant, bring up their guns, and pound the open plain down below to both east and south, causing Foch's entire position to crumble. The French narrowly averted this catastrophic outcome. Sealing off the German incursion, largely by artillery fire, they launched a series of costly counter-attacks to try to recapture the *château*. In the evening, after an epic defence, the Germans finally abandoned Mondement and retreated.

The intriguing question is how the Germans managed to seize such a strong position in the first place. Responsibility for holding this area rested with the *Division du Maroc*. Its commander, *Général de brigade* Georges Humbert, ordered the regiment that was at Mondement to entrench outside the village, so as to avoid unnecessary losses from the heavy German bombardment of the houses. But

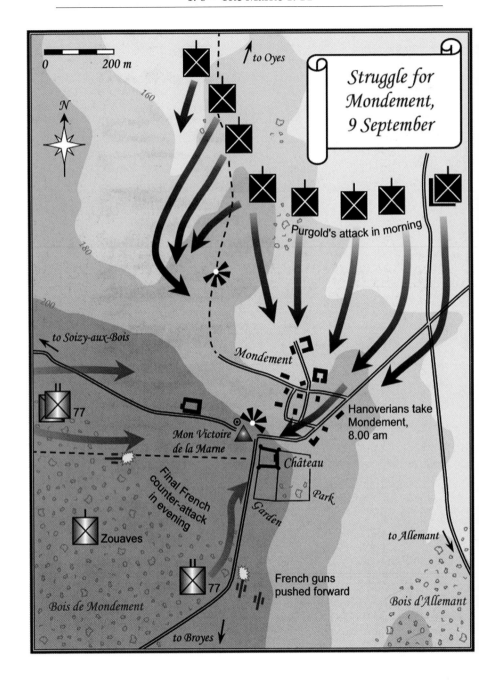

0   200 m

N

to Oyes

Struggle for Mondement, 9 September

Purgold's attack in morning

to Soizy-aux-Bois

160

180

200

Mondement

77

Mon Victoire de la Marne

Hanoverians take Mondement, 8.00 am

Final French counter-attack in evening

Château

Garden

Park

Zouaves

to Allemant

77

French guns pushed forward

Bois de Mondement

Bois d'Allemant

to Broyes

The northern side of the **château**.

misunderstandings resulted in a failure to organize the position properly. Most crucially of all, the *château* – the main stronghold, situated at the upper edge of the village – was left without a garrison. Coordination also broke down on the German side, as tiredness was reducing the efficiency of staffwork in both armies. By nightfall on the 8th the Germans had established themselves on the southern side of the St-Gond marshes, but still needed to capture the crucial high ground at Mondement, which dominated their low-lying positions. An attack, originally scheduled for the evening of the 8th, was postponed, but not all units were informed of the change. As a result of the confusion, *Infanterie-Regiment Nr 164* ended up attacking on its own on the morning of the 9th.

Storming Mondement

To reach Mondement, the Hanoverians had to advance 2 km, first crossing the exposed low ground near the marshes and then climbing uphill to the top of the heights. Two battalions under *Hauptmann* Edgar Purgold made the attack, accompanied by four machine-guns, while the third battalion waited in reserve at Oyes. The advance began shortly before 5.00 am, just after it had become light enough to see. Crucially, a thick mist drifted over the marshes, providing some badly needed cover.

Purgold's leading elements entered Mondement village towards 8.00 am, three hours after beginning the advance from Oyes. After surprising the French outposts about 1 km north of Mondement, the Hanoverians had worked their way forward by bounds, covered by the rifle-fire of their comrades. When the attack became pinned down some 500 metres short of its objective, Purgold sent a sketch of the French positions back to his regimental commander at Oyes, asking for reinforcements and artillery support. Meanwhile, his

The German view of Mondement.

losses continued to mount, but the firepower of his four machine-guns managed to break the deadlock. Purgold urged his men on across the final hollow separating them from Mondement. *Leutnant* Karl Gabler vividly recalled the bedlam that ensued. 'As we ran down, we came under an insane rifle and artillery fire', he wrote. 'It was like a *Hexenkessel* [a witches' cauldron], with the shots whistling and thundering around us.' Another soldier, Wilhelm Dörnte, could see barely 10 metres to either side, because of all the dust and smoke. He heard a scream as a man was wounded, and crawled over, but was powerless to do more than bandage him as best he could. 'Dear God, make it quick', Dörnte prayed. 'But don't leave me lying badly hurt in this hell.'

Various groups of men seized different parts of the village. A detachment stormed its way through to the *château*, the biggest prize of

Tower at the north-western angle of the **château.**

all, and found that it contained barely any defenders. The Hanoverians broke into the grounds through breaches in the northern wall of the enclosures, where it had been hit by shellfire. Immediately, they began preparing the *château* for defence, piercing loopholes, closing the main gates and blocking up the windows with mattresses. Purgold's position was precarious. He was effectively cut off, as the French artillery had turned the valley floor behind him into a sea of bursting shells. Elements of Humbert's division had blocked the road south from Mondement to Broyes, and were probing the Hanoverian positions. At 9.00 am a section of *zouaves* penetrated into the grounds of the *château* before being repelled. Casualties continued to whittle down Purgold's force. He himself was wounded in the belly, but remained in command for the rest of the day. At 10.45 am he sent a message to the rear, demanding support. 'Reinforcement vital, or else the village can not be held', it read. 'Ammunition very necessary, especially for machine guns.' In response, a cart galloped through the French fire with food and ammunition, and took four or five wounded men away on its return trip. But it proved impossible to get reinforcements through: the shellfire was so intense that those German units that did try to cross the exposed ground from Oyes were quickly pinned down.

For the moment the situation was one of stalemate. Humbert's units were too depleted and dispersed to retake Mondement unaided. In reponse to his appeal for help, he was sent the crack *77e régiment*, but it had to march from the vicinity of Linthes, 6–8 km to the southeast. In the meantime, as the *42e division* passed behind Mondement to strengthen Foch's eastern wing, it temporarily detached its artillery and two battalions of *chasseurs à pied* to help contain the German incursion.

Once the *77e* arrived towards the end of the morning, Humbert was able to counter-attack in earnest. The first step was to secure the area by firmly occupying the two woods on either side of Mondement. To do this, the *77e* was split into two parts. Two battalions were sent into the *Bois de Mondement* in the west, while the third, under *Commandant* Philippe de Beaufort, entered the *Bois d'Allemant* in the east.

Once the woods were secure, the objective became the recapture of Mondement. But time was not on the French side. Humbert was under pressure to throw the Germans back quickly, because of the increasingly desperate situation of the *9e armée* in the plain further east.

'For France – charge!'

Beaufort had now occupied the *Bois d'Allemant* with his battalion of the *77e*. The *château* was just 500 metres to the north-west, but stood on the eastern edge of the escarpment. A direct attack was out of the question, as it would have had to cross an exposed gully. Instead, Beaufort attacked from the south, along the Broyes–Mondement road (the D45), which runs through the woods along the top of the escarpment. The *77e* came from the town of Cholet, in the staunchly Catholic region of western France. Beaufort had one of his men – a priest in civilian life – give absolution to the battalion. The men knelt. Then, at 2.30 pm, Beaufort gave the order to advance. 'Forwards, my children!' he called. 'For France – charge!'

The attack was a bloody failure. The need for haste had limited the preliminary artillery bombardment to just ten minutes, and the French lacked the heavy guns they needed for this task. Their 75mm pieces managed to knock two or three breaches in the garden wall, but were powerless to do much damage to the *château* itself, which was largely shielded from observation by the woods. Beaufort himself was shot through the head, and his men were exposed to a hail of bullets from the defenders. 'We distributed ourselves between the windows,' explained a Hanoverian soldier, 'where we limited our losses as much as possible by sheltering behind tables, chairs, silk beds, and other objects, while inflicting as much damage as possible on the enemy.' The survivors of Beaufort's battalion rallied behind the southern wall of the enclosure, and then fell back to the cover of the woods. The other two battalions of the *77e* heard the sounds of Beaufort's assault and hurriedly launched a separate attack. Charging against the village of Mondement from the west, they, too, were repelled.

Undaunted, Humbert ordered the *77e* to try again. This time a properly coordinated attack was prepared for 6.30 pm. All three battalions of the *77e* would make a simultaneous assault on the village and the *château*, supported by Humbert's *zouaves*. Three 75mm guns were brought right forward to soften up the defences from

*The **77e régiment** attacks the **château**.*

close range. Two were placed on the road south of the *château*, hidden amid the woods, from where they could be pushed out of cover, round the final bend in the road, to open fire at a range of just 300 metres. The other gun was rolled by hand to a distance of 400 metres west of the *château*, opposite the entrance gate.

From 6.00 pm the French shells started hitting the *château* and some of the roofs caught fire. Purgold now ordered his men to abandon Mondement, having learned that the rest of his regiment at Oyes was preparing to fall back – this was part of the more general German retreat that was the result of their defeat in the Battle of the Marne as a whole. By 6.45 pm the last of the garrison had left the *château*. Shortly afterwards the *77e* broke in through the main gate and the breaches of the garden wall, without having to fire a shot.

WHAT TO SEE

The tour is designed for walking, but since its starting point, the village of Oyes, has limited car parking, it is best to drive the first stretch and then park at Mondement. As you head south from Oyes along the road to Mondement, you are following the axis of Purgold's attack on the morning of the 9th. The Hanoverians – barely 900 of them in all – advanced parallel to this road, with their companies arrayed along a 1-km front across the fields to the west. Above you, on the horizon, a colossal monument marks their objective.

The ascent of the escarpment brings you to a crossroads. Turn right on to the D45 and cover the final 350 metres up to the village of Mondement. This is the route taken by Purgold's easternmost companies in the final stages of their attack. After passing through the village you reach the top of the plateau, with the *château* on your left. Stop at the car park in front of the church, so you can walk around.

Point 1: The *château*

Solid, stone walls make the *château* a formidable strongpoint. At the time of the battle it was even stronger than it appears today, for the courtyard was completely enclosed by a combination of the railings alongside the road and buildings on the other three sides. The southern wing, which was particularly badly damaged during the action, was later demolished.

The *château* is private property and not open to the public, but the action can be followed easily enough from outside. Set into the

*Inside the courtyard of the **château** after the battle.*

*The **château**'s courtyard today.*

*The French President, Raymond Poincaré, visits the **château** on the third anniversary of the battle. The walls are still pock-marked, but the main building has now been temporarily repaired with a zinc roof. Poincaré is the central figure. To the left of him is the Premier, Alexandre Ribot (tall, with a white beard). They are followed by Joffre, in a dark uniform.*

Humbert, commander of the **Division du Maroc***.*

wall, on the right of the railings, is a stone engraved with an image of Humbert, the commander of the *Division du Maroc*. The inscription is a tribute from Foch: 'People have heard of the dogged defence of Mondement – the indispensable pivot of our resistance. Humbert was its soul.' Until the 9th Humbert had successfully held this sector, and it was he who organized the recapture of the *château* after its fall.

Point 2: The monument
Towering over the area is the remarkable monument to the victory of the Marne. Over 35 metres tall, it rests on foundations sunk as deep as 22 metres. The design was inspired by the standing stones

The monument to the victory of the Marne.

erected by the ancient Celts. It stands at the highwater mark of the German advance and is dedicated, as an inscription at the rear attests, 'to all those who, since the most ancient times, have raised a boundary stone on our land against the invader.' Begun in 1931, the monument was largely complete by the end of 1932, apart from the decorative sculptures. But the expense of the structure matched its scale, the necessary funds ran out and work was abandoned early in 1933. Not until five years later was the monument finally finished. Even then, the inauguration – initially scheduled for September 1939 – was cancelled because of the Second World War, and was held only in 1951.

Although the monument looks like a solid block of stone, it is actually made from reinforced concrete and has a hollow core. The colour was deliberately chosen to reflect that of the famous rose sandstone from the Vosges mountains above the Rhine river, and it therefore underlines the fact that France had regained her lost province of Alsace as a result of the war. The bas-reliefs at the foot of the monument depict Joffre and a French soldier in the centre, flanked by the Allied army commanders in the order in which they stood in the battle. From east to west, you can identify: Sarrail (3e armée); Langle de Cary (4e armée); Foch (9e armée); Franchet d'Espèrey (5e armée); Sir John French (BEF); Maunoury (6e armée); and Galliéni, the military governor of Paris. 'At Joffre's command', reads an inscription, 'the French army, which was in full retreat, halted and turned to face the enemy. The Battle of the Marne then opened on a front of 70 leagues, from Verdun to the gates of Paris. After several days of heroic fighting, the enemy everywhere retreated, and victory passed all along the front.' Near the top of the monument a winged figure of victory flies through the sky. The monument is also inscribed with Joffre's order of the day of 6 September (page 193). From the front of the monument a magnificent view extends over the St-Gond marshes.

Point 3: The church
The nearby churchyard contains four commemorative plaques and a mass grave. Most of the soldiers who fell at Mondement were later reinterred in cemeteries elsewhere, but some remain here. The reason we know their names is that on the morning after the battle a subaltern of the 77e régiment recorded them on a wall inside the church, and drew a sketch of where the men had been buried. You can still see his graffiti today, on the left as you face the altar.

Mondement church, seen from the monument.

Point 4: The museum

A small museum about the battle is housed in the *mairie* towards the eastern end of the village. (Follow the signpost from the church that reads *accès musée*.) The remarkable relics include a French cavalryman's corroded helmet, which was found in the St-Gond marshes. Bear in mind when planning your trip that the museum's opening times are very limited (page 208). Plans are being made to transfer part of the museum to Soizy-aux-Bois, 4 km to the north-west, in time for the centenary of the battle.

Circular walk

To see Mondement from the German perspective, take the track from the north-western corner of Mondement village. It heads along a spur protruding northwards from the escarpment, and commands

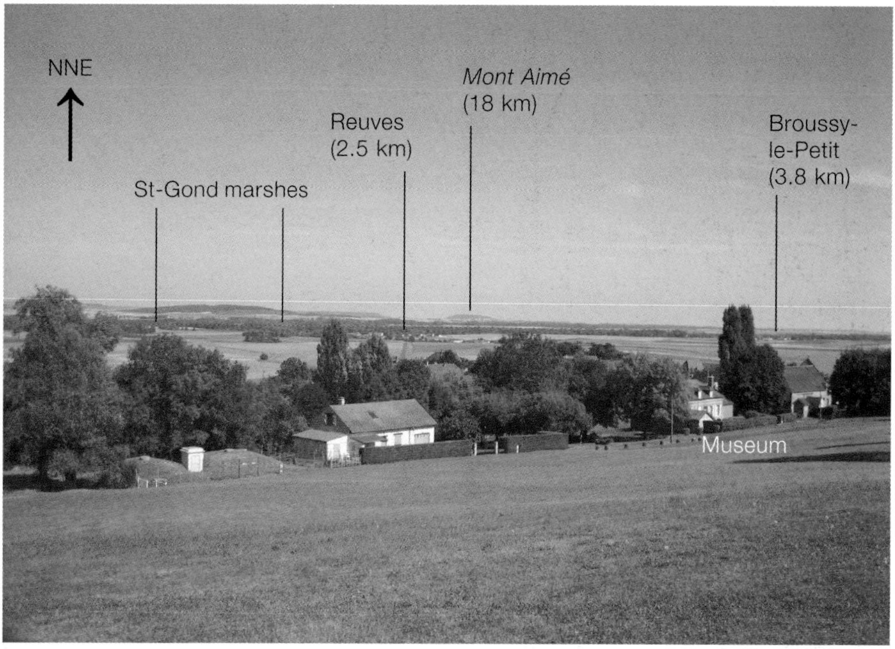

NNE

St-Gond marshes

Reuves
(2.5 km)

Mont Aimé
(18 km)

Broussy-
le-Petit
(3.8 km)

Museum

The view from the monument.

superb views in all directions. The track leads you towards Oyes, from where you can return to Mondement by road. It is useful to have a 1:25,000 scale map for this walk, which is 7 km long.

Optional visits

If time permits, visit the French military cemetery at Soizy-aux-Bois, where almost 1,700 men are buried in a couple of mass graves. You may also wish to see Broyes and Allemant, 3 km south of Mondement, for spectacular views from the edge of the escarpment. Below you is the plain crossed by the *42e division* in the afternoon of 9 September, as it marched to bolster Foch's crumbling right wing (page 151). At Broyes the *Château des Pucelles* was Humbert's command post from 7 September, and now houses the *mairie*.

FURTHER AFIELD

To supplement the battlefield tours, the following are some individual points of interest.

Dormans

Dormans lies in the Marne valley, 98 km east of Paris, and contains a grandiose memorial to the First and Second Battles of the Marne, two of the most pivotal German defeats of the war. The second battle began on 15 July 1918, when the Germans launched what

Dormans: the memorial to the two Battles of the Marne.

turned out to be their last great offensive on the Western Front. They managed to cross the Marne at Dormans, gaining a bridgehead 6 km deep on the south bank before they were stopped. The Allies under Foch began a counter-attack on the 18th, and over the next three weeks reduced the German salient, winning a clear-cut victory that turned the tide of the war.

Begun in 1920, the *Mémorial des batailles de la Marne* took eleven years to build. It consists of the main building – a chapel and its crypt – linked by a cloister to an ossuary holding the remains of over 1,300 French soldiers. This is one of France's four great national monuments on the Western Front (the others being the Douaumont ossuary at Verdun, the Hartmannswillerkopf in the Vosges and Notre-Dame de Lorette in the Pas-de-Calais). Inside the chapel, climb the tower for superb views over the Marne valley. In the town itself, 700 metres north of the memorial, a military cemetery contains another 4,000 French and German dead.

Montmirail

The town of Montmirail is 88 km east of Paris. On the evening of 8 September it witnessed one of the decisive actions of the Battle of the Marne, when the French *5e armée* seized the nearby village of Marchais under the cover of darkness. Marchais stood on the right flank of the German *2. Armee*, and had a dominating position on high ground 4 km north-west of Montmirail. Its capture therefore forced the *2. Armee* to fall back north-eastwards, and irreversibly widened the gap between it and the *1. Armee*.

Montmirail is all the more interesting in that it was the scene of one of Napoleon's victories during his 1814 campaign. To commemorate that victory, a column was erected on the battlefield in 1866. You will find it 1.75 km east of Marchais, on the northern side of the D933. Look closely at the column and you will see a dent about one-third of the way up, made by a shell during the Battle of the Marne.

On the opposite side of the road is another link between the two battles. A monument remembers the Montmirail *promotion* of the French officer training school, the *Ecole spéciale militaire de St-Cyr*. The *promotion* (a group of cadets passing out together in the same

192 • The Marne 1914

year) was named in honour of the centenary of Napoleon's victory, and according to the inscription on the monument as many as 233 of its members died for France between 1914 and 1955. (The exact figure has been disputed, but amounts to about half of the *promotion*.)

The cadets were due to be appointed *sous-lieutenants* on 1 August 1914. On the day before, with war imminent, they supposedly swore an oath to wear the white gloves and the drooping red-and-white plume of a *St-Cyrien* for their first action. The oath of 1914 quickly passed into legend. In reality, it was sworn not by an entire *promotion*, but by a group of about thirty members of two *promotions*, and it remains unclear how many actually carried out this act of bravado on the battlefield. The writer André Thérive – himself a veteran of 1914 – cast doubt on it. 'As regards the plumes', he wrote, 'they would have provoked too much laughter.' He pointed out how unlikely it was that anyone would have alerted the newly commissioned officers that they were about to come under fire: 'Listen up! You need to put on your gloves now, because the *Boches* are going to fire over you, and these beetroots are the field of honour.' Yet the courage of the *St-Cyriens* has never been doubted: over 5,500 of them died for France during the First World War.

Bar-sur-Aube

Bar-sur-Aube lies 189 km east-south-east of Paris, and on the eve of the battle was the location of Joffre's headquarters, or *Grand-quartier-général* (GQG). Joffre had previously been based at the central location of Vitry-le-François, but on 1 September, as the German advance drew closer, GQG had moved 56 km further south to Bar-sur-Aube.

Joffre was billeted at the *Château du Jard*, which you will find at 29, *avenue du Général Leclerc* (the D619). The *château* is on the left-hand side of the road as it heads out of town to the north-west. Joffre had an office 500 metres away at GQG, which had been established in the *Ecole Arthur Bureau* (midway between the town centre and the railway station, in the *rue du Maréchal Joffre*).

During Joffre's stay at Bar-sur-Aube, the most momentous day came on 4 September. The vulnerability of the Germans to a counter-offensive was by now obvious from the situation map, but every-thing depended on the right timing. On reaching GQG around 6.30 that morning Joffre found his staff divided as to what should be done. Some officers wanted to strike immediately, rather than fall back as far as the Seine, but *Général de brigade* Henri Berthelot, the assistant chief of staff in charge of operations, favoured waiting until the Germans had advanced deeper into the trap.

This was the key decision, and it lay with Joffre. He tended to make up his mind not in a sudden flash of genius but by slowly pondering a problem. While saying little himself, he listened to proposals and then carefully weighed up the options, turning an idea over and over until it had matured. Discussions continued during the day, and since it was hot Joffre spent much of his time in the schoolyard outside GQG, sitting in the shade of a weeping ash tree. That evening the pieces finally fell into place. Confirmation arrived that both the *5e* and *9e armées* would be ready to attack as early as the 6th. Furthermore, the commander of the former, Franchet d'Espèrey, had met the BEF's deputy chief of staff and had produced a provisional plan for an offensive. Then came a telephone call from Galliéni, the military governor of Paris. One of the great myths of the battle is that Galliéni had to convince a reluctant Joffre to attack. In reality, Joffre had already made that decision, and Galliéni's call did no more than confirm the details. Joffre's directive for an offensive on the 6th – the *Ordre général no. 6* – was now finalized, and signed by him at 10.00 pm.

Next day, 5 September, GQG moved 40 km further south to Châtillon-sur-Seine. In fact, the move was unnecessary now that the retreat had ended, but since the preparations had already been made, it went ahead anyway. As a result, it was from Châtillon that Joffre issued his famous order of the day to mark the start of the Marne offensive. It was a rare, direct appeal to his troops:

> Now that a battle is beginning on which the fate of our country depends, it is important to remind all ranks that there must be no more looking to the rear. Every effort must be made to attack and drive back the enemy. Units unable to advance further must hold the conquered ground whatever the cost, and die where they stand rather than fall back. In the present circumstances, no weakness can be tolerated.

The message was drafted on the evening of the 5th, not by Joffre personally but by his staff. He himself simply approved it, after making a few changes. It was brief and blunt, because time was short, and because a longer explanation of the situation was unnecessary. It caught the solemnity of the moment. 'Yes,' reflected a French gunner when the order was read to his battery, 'we have understood. We would never have been able to express our innermost thoughts so simply and completely.'

The order was telephoned to the various army headquarters at the last moment, to ensure that no fore-warning of the offensive reached the Germans. (In the event, they found a copy on the battlefield by the end of 6 September, and so Moltke soon gained confirmation that the attacks were a major offensive, launched in earnest.) The late issue of the order meant that some French units received it, if at all, only in mid-battle. One infantryman, *Capitaine* Jean Charbonneau, felt that its real impact was on the various commanders and staff officers, among whom it fostered a new mood by making clear Joffre's intent. 'But,' he added, 'and I may be about to shatter some illusions here, I do not think that this stirring order of the day seriously influenced the troops themselves.' The men of his regiment in the *4e armée* heard it only on the morning of the 8th, after they had been relieved from the front line. 'Don't think that we scorned the words or the delivery. But by then, it was primarily the business of the comrades who had taken our place in the line. Besides, on the day after a fight, you prefer not to think of anything, nor to consider big issues. Each day has problems enough of its own.' In fact, Charbonneau was convinced that the morale of the men was boosted more by what they personally witnessed. Listening to the bark of French 75mm guns, and watching the destruction wrought by their shells, was an obvious example, but even small and seemingly insignificant incidents could be psychologically important – such as the sight of a German cavalry horse in poor condition.

Vaux-le-Pénil

The *Château de Vaux-le-Pénil* in the outskirts of Melun, 43 km southeast of Paris, was Sir John French's headquarters at the start of the Battle of the Marne. It hosted a dramatic meeting between him and Joffre on the eve of the battle. Even after Joffre had signed the *Ordre*

Château de Vaux-le-Pénil.

général no. 6 in the evening of 4 September (page 193), the BEF's readiness to participate in his counter-offensive remained uncertain. Hence, Joffre personally visited Vaux-le-Pénil on the afternoon of the 5th and secured the BEF's cooperation by making an emotional appeal to its commander.

The *château* stands on the right bank of the Seine, 1 km south-east of the centre of Melun. Approach it along the *rue de la Libération* from the northern outskirts of Vaux-le-Pénil. Note the plaque fixed to a pillar beside the entrance gate. The inscription is misleading: Joffre and Sir John French did not, in fact, take a joint decision for a counter-offensive. Joffre had already made that decision, and Sir John was simply persuaded to conform. The *château* is not normally open to the public, although rooms are hired out for events. You can see the rear of the building, through a gap in the trees, from the road running alongside the Seine.

Paris

The Eiffel Tower is actually a key relic of the battle, as the French used it to broadcast and intercept radio messages. Some 150 metres south-east of the Tower's southern pillar, amid the trees on the *Champ de Mars*, is a monument to *Général de division* Gustave Ferrié, a pioneer in French military radio communications. Before the war he had carried out crucial experiments in wireless telegraphy, using the Tower to support the antennae.

The victory of the Marne probably saved the Tower from being destroyed. On 2 September, as the Germans neared Paris, the new military governor, Galliéni, sought confirmation from the Minister of War whether the city was to be held, with all the devastation that might entail. The Minister replied that it was to be defended *à outrance* ('to the bitter end'). Preparations were made to blow up the wireless station at the Eiffel Tower if that became necessary, and the Tower itself might well have shared the same fate.

At the south-eastern end of the *Champ de Mars*, in front of the *Ecole militaire*, is a bronze statue of Joffre on horseback. Inaugurated in 1939, it faces a similar one of Foch, sited on the *place du Trocadéro* on the far side of the Seine. Galliéni is commemorated by a statue on the *place Vauban* on the southern side of the *Hôtel des Invalides*. This was actually the second statue of Galliéni to be commissioned as a tribute from the city of Paris. The first was thought to be unsatisfactory, and was consigned to the countryside outside Meaux (page 47). The replacement was inaugurated in 1926, and initially stood on the esplanade in front of the *Invalides*, but was moved to its current location to make way for the *Exposition internationale* of 1937. Galliéni's statue now looks in the direction of the *Lycée Victor-Duruy*, a school 250 metres to the east on the *boulevard des Invalides*, where (as a plaque records) he had his headquarters during the Battle of the Marne.

Inside the *Hôtel des Invalides* is the French army museum, the *Musée de l'armée*, and also the *Eglise du Dôme*, where you will find the tombs of both Foch and Napoleon. In contrast to this grandiose setting, Joffre was buried, at his own request, at *La Châtaigneraie*, his home at Louveciennes, 17 km west of the centre of Paris. It is a private residence, not open to the public, but the entrance gateway has a commemorative plaque. Joffre's mausoleum is visible in the grounds of the house: go down the side-road (the *chemin des Gressets*), following the signs for the *mausolée*, and look over the gate. Louveciennes can be reached by train from the *Gare St-Lazare*, and Joffre's residence is 1 km south-west of the local railway station, at 25, *rue du Maréchal Joffre*.

Taxis of the Marne

The story of how taxi-cabs were used to rush French reinforcements to the battlefield has been elevated into legend. The basic facts are more down to earth. Joffre withdrew several corps from his more easterly armies to strengthen his western wing for the battle. Among them was the *4e corps*, which was transported by railway from the Argonne area (190 km from Paris) to reinforce the *6e armée*. But the arrival of this corps' *7e division* at the capital was delayed by congestion. The division was not ready to be committed to action until 7 September, and was needed next morning on the northern sector of the Battlefield of the Ourcq, more than 30 km away. Some elements were sent by train north-eastwards to Nanteuil-le-Haudouin, but road transport was also needed, partly as it was feared that sections of the railway tracks might have been destroyed.

On the evening of 6 September requisitioned taxis were assembled on the esplanade in front of the *Hôtel des Invalides*. The situation was confused at first, but the mission was clarified on the 7th. More taxis were requisitioned that day, and in the evening two convoys picked up five battalions of the *7e division* from an area 14 km east of Paris. The taxis then headed north-eastwards, through Dammartin, and unloaded their passengers between Nanteuil and Silly-le-Long in the early hours of the 8th. The *7e division* was able to intervene in the battle that same morning.

This minor incident of the battle was exaggerated out of all proportion. In reality, the 4,000 men transported by taxi were a minute, insignificant fraction of those under Joffre's command. Transporting the *4e corps* by railway to Paris was actually more important than the subsequent use of taxis to shift just part of one of its divisions to the battlefield. It was the trains – far more than any taxis – that did most to win the Marne.

The use of taxis, or other civilian vehicles, was not even a new idea: Napoleon had regularly hired waggons to transport soldiers across France a full century earlier. The inescapable fact is that taxis were not the most suitable vehicles, since their limited capacity required too many drivers to transport troops in large numbers. They were pressed into service only because buses and vans had already been requisitioned for supporting the armies in the field.

The taxis of the Marne did have an important impact, but on the French population's morale, rather than on the outcome of the battle. The idea of civilian taxi-drivers helping the army embodied the *Union sacrée*, the spirit of national cohesion that replaced the bitter social divisions of pre-war France, when the army had been distrusted by many on the left as a tool for repression. As a symbol of this new national unity, the taxis became a potent myth.

Where to see the taxi memorials
Reminders of the taxis can be found in and around Paris. One of the actual vehicles used in the battle, a Renault AG-1, is on display at the *Musée de l'armée* at the *Hôtel des Invalides*. Another taxi of the type used in 1914 can be seen in the *Musée de la Grande guerre* at Meaux (page 50). Many of the taxi companies in 1914 were based at Levallois-Perret, 7 km north-west of the centre of Paris, and an impressive marble memorial now stands in the *place 11 novembre 1918*. You can reach Levallois-Perret by taking *Métro* Line 3 to its terminus, *Pont de Levallois Bécon*.

Most of the other memorials are in the eastern suburbs of Paris, where the taxis collected their troops. In 1914 the towns in this area were surrounded by countryside, but have now been absorbed by the sprawling capital. Start at Gagny, which you can reach by rapid-transit train on *RER* Line E2. This was where the second convoy picked up the *103e régiment*. A plaque commemorating these events could be found until recently outside the *Hôtel de ville*, but it was removed when the building was renovated. Plans are afoot to redevelop the adjacent square by creating an underground car-park, following which the taxis plaque will be reinstalled. In the meantime the memory of the taxis is preserved in the municipal coat of arms, which incorporates three silver taxi wheels, and in Gagny's motto, *Exierunt mille ad victoriam* ('a thousand set out to victory'). This is a reference to the number of taxis supposedly involved in the

Taxis monument at Levallois-Perret.

operation, although the total in both convoys combined was actually nearer 600.

Another memorial exists at Le Raincy, 2 km north-west of Gagny. From the *RER* station, walk 750 metres northwards along the *avenue de la Résistance* to the *Eglise Notre-Dame*, which you will find on the left at number 83. The church was built in 1922–3 to honour the fallen of the Battle of the Marne. As you enter, note the stained-glass window on the left. Known as the *Vierge aux taxis*, it is dedicated to the Virgin Mary. Several taxis can be seen in the centre, and among the figures on the left are Galliéni, Foch and Maunoury.

Walk 150 metres further along the *avenue de la Résistance* and you will find the *Mémorial municipal*, where the *allée de Montfermeil* turns off to the right. Note the scenes carved at the base of the memorial, including the taxi on the right. The *Hôtel de ville* of Le Raincy, where Maunoury (the commander of the *6e armée*) had his headquarters at the start of the battle, is a further 150 metres along the *avenue de la Résistance*, and contains a bust of him in the lobby.

Gagny was the pick-up point only for the second taxi convoy. The first collected the men of the *104e régiment* from a location called the *Barrière de Livry* at the town of Livry-Gargan. It was a convenient spot, for it was on the main road, the N3, that ran eastwards out of Paris. Today the place is marked by a plaque, half-concealed in a flower-bed, on the *avenue Charles de Gaulle*, at the northern corner of the crossroads of the N3 and N370. (From the church at Le Raincy it is a 3-km walk to the north-east along the D116, or you can catch *Bus Optile 605*, which runs along the same road.)

At the village of Tremblay-Vieux-Pays, 1 km south of Charles de Gaulle airport, another plaque is on the green in front of the church. (The village is marked on some maps as Le Petit Tremblay, and can be reached by catching *Bus Optile 91* from Vert Galant station on *RER* Line B5.) The plaque records that on the night of 6/7 September 500 Parisian taxis assembled here. This is a reminder of the confusion that preceded the operation: the first convoy was initially sent to Tremblay but eventually picked up its troops at the *Barrière de Livry*.

Finally a memorial stone at Nanteuil-le-Haudouin, 45 km northeast of the centre of Paris, commemorates the disembarkation of the troops at the end of their journey. The memorial is beside the roundabout at the south-western entrance to the town, where the *rue de Paris* (from Silly-Le-Long) crosses the *rue de Lizy*.

FURTHER READING

What follows is a selection of the most interesting books about the battle. For reasons of space, only a handful of regimental histories have been mentioned, but many others, both British and German, contain a wealth of information. Histories of French regiments rarely go into much detail, but the unit war diaries, or *journaux des marches et operations*, are often useful and can be consulted on the *Mémoire des hommes* website (page 208).

Battlefield guides
Guidebooks devoted specifically to the battlefield are almost non-existent. The obvious exception is the Michelin guide, *Battle-fields of the Marne, 1914*, first published in 1917, yet it ignores the British actions. In 2011 Michelin published a French-language guide, *Les champs de bataille: la Marne et la Champagne*, which does cover some of the BEF's operations but omits part of Foch's sector. Details of the BEF's actions can be found in the British War Office's *Battle of the Marne, 8th–10th September, 1914: tour of the battlefield*, published in 1935.

Historical background
Herwig, Holger H. *The Marne, 1914*. New York, 2009.
Sumner, Ian. *The First Battle of the Marne, 1914*. Oxford, 2010.
Tuchman, Barbara W. *The guns of August*. 1962. Reissued New York, 2004.
Tyng, Sewell T. *The campaign of the Marne, 1914*. 1935. Reissued Yardley, 2007.

Official histories
Edmonds, Sir James Edward. *Military operations, France and Belgium, 1914: Mons, the retreat to the Seine, the Marne and the Aisne, August–October 1914*, 3rd ed. 1933. Reissued London, 1992.

France: Ministère de la guerre. *Les armées françaises dans la Grande guerre*, 11 tomes. Paris, 1922–37. Tome 1, vol 3.

Germany: Reichsarchiv. *Der Weltkrieg, 1914 bis 1918*, 15 vols. Berlin, 1925–44. Vol. 4.

The *Reichsarchiv* also published more detailed, supplementary studies in 1928, under the title *Das Marnedrama 1914*, as volumes 22 to 26 of the *Schlachten des Weltkrieges*.

Tour 1: Opening clash

Aldrich, Mildred. *A hilltop on the Marne, being letters written June 3–September 8, 1914.* New York, 1915.

Germany: Reichsarchiv. *Schlachten des Weltkrieges*, vol. 26. Berlin, 1928.

Juin, Alphonse-Pierre. *La Brigade marocaine à la bataille de la Marne.* Paris, 1964.

Koeltz, Marie-Louis. *L'armée von Kluck à la bataille de la Marne.* Paris, 1931.

Michel, René. *Un combat de rencontre.* Paris, 1931.

Tuffrau, Paul. *1914–1918: quatre années sur le front, carnets d'un combattant.* Paris, 1998.

Wirth, Alfred. *Von der Saale zur Aisne.* Leipzig, nd.

Tour 2: Battle of the Ourcq

von Brandis, Cordt. *Die vom Douaumont: das Ruppiner Regiment 24 im Weltkrieg.* Berlin, 1930.

[This regimental history can be supplemented with two volumes of Brandis' personal recollections: *Die Stürmer von Douaumont* (published in 1917, and reissued in 1934), and *Vor uns der Douaumont: aus dem Leben eines altern Soldaten* (published in 1966).]

Germany: Reichsarchiv. *Schlachten des Weltkrieges*, vol. 26. Berlin, 1928.

Heubner, Heinrich. *Unter Emmich vor Lüttich, unter Kluck vor Paris.* Schwerin, 1915.

Koeltz (listed under Tour 1).

Lintier, Paul. *My 75: reminiscences of a gunner.* 1917. Reissued Solihull, 2012.

Lohrisch, Hermann. *In Siegessturm von Lüttich an die Marne.* Leipzig, 1917.

Mallet, Christian. *Impressions and experiences of a French trooper.* London, 1916.

Marbeau, Emmanuel. *Souvenirs de Meaux: avant, pendant et après la bataille de la Marne.* 1915. Reissued Montceaux-les-Meaux, 2007.

Smart, Mary. *A flight with fame: the life and art of Frederick MacMonnies.* Madison, 1996.

Tuffrau (listed under Tour 1).

Tour 3: Joffre's offensive

von Brandis (listed under Tour 2).

Durosoir, Luc (ed.). *Deux musiciens dans la Grande guerre: Lucien Durosoir et Maurice Maréchal.* Paris, 2005.

Germany: Reichsarchiv. *Schlachten des Weltkrieges,* vol. 22. Berlin, 1928.

Grasset, Alphonse. *La bataille des deux Morins.* Paris, 1934.

Heubner (listed under Tour 2).

La Chaussée, J. *De Charleroi à Verdun dans l'infanterie.* Paris, 1933.

Mangin, Charles. *Des hommes et des faits.* Paris, 1923.

Pedroncini, Guy. *Pétain [vol. 1]: le soldat et la gloire.* Paris, 1989.

Salle, Général. 'Le 129e régiment d'infanterie à Courgivaux et à Montmirail', in *Les archives de la Grande guerre* (1922), année 4, tome 14, pp. 1320–35.

Smith, Leonard V. *Between mutiny and obedience: the case of the French Fifth Infantry Division during World War I.* Princeton, NJ, 1994.

Williams, Charles. *Pétain.* London, 2005.

Tour 4: The British advance

von Alten, Hans, et al. *Geschichte des Garde-Schützen-Bataillons.* Berlin, 1928.

Anon. 'Diary of a subaltern', in *Blackwood's magazine* (Jan–Jun 1915), vol. 197, no. 1191, pp. 1–18; and no. 1192, pp. 141–55. [The author served in the 1/The King's (Liverpool Regiment).]

Coleman, Frederic. *From Mons to Ypres with French.* London, 1916.

Craster, J.M. (ed.). *'Fifteen rounds a minute': the Grenadiers at war.* London, 1976.

Germany: Army. *Garde-Jäger-Bataillon.* Oldenburg, 1934.

Great Britain: War Office. *Battle of the Marne, 8th–10th September, 1914: tour of the battlefield.* London, 1935.

Jourdain, Henry, and Edward Fraser, *The Connaught Rangers*, 3 vols. London, 1924–8. Vol. 1.

Tour 5: Forcing the Marne
Corns, Cathryn, and John Hughes-Wilson. *Blindfold and alone: British military executions in the Great War*. London, 2001.

Dunn, James. *The war the infantry knew*. 1938. Reissued London, 1987.

Germany: Reichsarchiv. *Schlachten des Weltkrieges*, vol. 26. Berlin, 1928.

Gleichen, Albert, Count. *The doings of the Fifteenth Infantry Brigade*. London, 1917.

Great Britain: War Office. *Battle of the Marne, 8th–10th September, 1914: tour of the battlefield*. London, 1935.

Hopkinson, Edward. *Spectamur agendo: 1st Battalion the East Lancashire Regiment, August and September, 1914*. Cambridge, 1926.

Richards, Frank. *Old soldiers never die*. 1933. Reissued London, 1964.

Roe, Edward. *Diary of an old contemptible*. Ed. by Peter Downham. Barnsley, 2004.

Smith-Dorrien, Sir Horace. *Memories of forty-eight years' service*. London, 1925.

Watkins, Owen Spencer. *With French in France and Flanders*. London, 1915.

Wyrall, Everard. *The history of the Duke of Cornwall's Light Infantry, 1914–1919*. London, 1932.

Young, B.K. 'The diary of an RE subaltern with the BEF in 1914', in *The Royal Engineers Journal* (1933), vol. 47, pp. 549–71.

Plans of the temporary bridge at La Ferté-sous-Jouarre can be found in the War Diary of the 9th Field Company RE (WO 95/1469), and in that of the CRE of the 4th Division (WO 95/1463). These can be consulted at The National Archives at Kew.

Tour 6: Foch's victory
Aston, Sir George. *The biography of the late Marshal Foch*. London, 1929.

Dubois, Alfred. *Deux ans de commandement sur le front de France, 1914–1916*, 2 vols. Paris, 1921. Vol. 1.

Foch, Ferdinand. *Des principes de la guerre*. 1903. Reissued Paris, 2007.

Foch, Ferdinand. *De la conduite de la guerre*. 1904. Reissued Paris, 2000.

Germany: Reichsarchiv. *Schlachten des Weltkrieges*, vols 24 and 25. Berlin, 1928.

Greenhalgh, Elizabeth. *Foch in command: the forging of a First World War general*. Cambridge, 2011.

Kleinhenz, Roland. 'La percée saxonne sur le front du centre', in Cochet, François (ed.). *Les batailles de la Marne: de l'Ourcq à Verdun, 1914 et 1918*. St-Cloud, 2004.

Koeltz, Marie-Louis. *D'Esternay aux marais de Saint-Gond*. Paris, 1930.

Le Goffic, Charles. *La Marne en feu*. Paris, 1921.

Lestien, G. 'L'action du Général Foch à la bataille de la Marne', in *Revue d'histoire de la guerre mondiale* (April 1930), 8th year, no. 2, pp. 113–41.

Monse, Rudolf. *Das 4. Kgl. Sächs. Infanterie-Regiment Nr. 103*. Bautzen, 1930.

Recouly, Raymond. *Foch: the winner of the war*. Trans. by Mary Cadwalader Jones. New York, 1920.

Réquin, Edouard. 'La journée du 9 septembre 1914 à la gauche de la 9e armée', in *Revue militaire française* (Oct–Dec 1930), vol. 37, pp. 214–44.

Tardieu, André. *Avec Foch, août-novembre 1914*. Paris, 1939.

Weygand, Jacques. *Weygand, mon père*. Paris, 1970.

Weygand, Maxime. *Foch*. Paris, 1947.

Be aware that Foch's *Mémoires pour servir à l'histoire de la guerre de 1914–1918*, 2 vols (published in 1931) were drafted by a ghost-writer.

Tour 7: The fight for Mondement

Chamard, Elie. *L'armée Foch à la Marne: la bataille de Mondement, septembre 1914*. Paris, 1939.

Germany: Reichsarchiv. *Schlachten des Weltkrieges*, vol. 25. Berlin, 1928.

Heeren, Dr, et al., *Geschichte des 4. Hannoverschen Infanterie-Regiments Nr. 164*. Hameln, 1932.

Further afield

Alexandre, Georges-René. *Avec Joffre d'Agadir à Verdun*. Paris, 1932.

Carré, Henri. *La véritable histoire des taxis de la Marne*. Paris, 1921.

Charbonneau, Jean. *La bataille des frontières et la bataille de la Marne*. Paris, 1928. [Useful for Joffre's order of the day.]

Germany: Reichsarchiv. *Schlachten des Weltkrieges*, vol. 23. Berlin, 1928. [Useful for Montmirail.]

Hirschauer, Auguste-Edouard, and Pierre Klein. *Paris en état de défense*. Paris, 1927.

Muller, Commandant. *Joffre et la Marne*. Paris, 1931.

Neiberg, Michael S. *The Second Battle of the Marne*. Bloomington, 2008.

Recouly, Raymond. *Joffre*, English trans. London, 1931.

German infantry at rest.

USEFUL ADDRESSES AND WEBSITES

We have not included museum opening times, as these are liable to change. Check on their websites for up-to-date details before finalizing your travel plans. The details below are valid as of September 2012.

Tourist information offices

Bar-sur-Aube: 4, *boulevard du 14 juillet* (www.tourisme.barsuraube.org)

Châlons-en-Champagne: 3, *quai des Arts* (www.chalons-tourisme.com)

Dormans: *Parc du château* (www.tourisme-dormans.fr)

Epernay: 7, *avenue de Champagne* (www.ot-epernay.fr)

La Ferté-sous-Jouarre: 34, *rue des Pelletiers* (www.la-ferte-sous-jouarre.fr)

Meaux: 1, *place Doumer* (www.tourisme-paysdemeaux.fr)

Melun: 18, *rue Paul Doumer* (www.ville-melun.fr)

Montmirail: 4, *place Rémy Petit* (www.montmirail-tourisme.eu)

Paris: *Office du tourisme de Paris* (www.parisinfo.com)
The main office is in the *1er arrondissement* at the heart of the city (25, *rue des Pyramides*), with additional information centres elsewhere, notably at three mainline railway stations (*Gares du Nord, de l'Est* and *de Lyon*).

Sézanne: *place de la République* (www.sezanne-tourisme.fr)

Troyes: 16, *blvd Carnot* (www.tourisme-troyes.com)

Départemental organisations:

Comité départemental du tourisme de l'Aube: 34, *quai Dampierre*, 1000 Troyes (www.aube-champagne.com)

Comité départemental du tourisme de la Marne: 13 *bis, rue Carnot*, 51000 Châlons-en-Champagne (www.tourisme-en-champagne.com)

Comité départemental du tourisme de Seine-et-Marne: 11, *rue Royale*, 77300 Fontainebleau (www.tourisme77.net)

French government tourist office:
This website includes important practical information for travelling in France.
United Kingdom: www.uk.franceguide.com
United States: www.us.franceguide.com

Museums and memorials
Dormans: *Mémorial des batailles de la Marne* (www.memorialdormans.free.fr)
Meaux: *Musée de la Grande guerre* (www.museedelagrandeguerre.eu)
Mondement: *Musée de Mondement* (www.mondement1914.asso.fr)
Villeroy: *Musée 1914–1918* (Email: museedevilleroy@yahoo.fr. Tel: 01 60 61 03 97)

Locating war graves
British: Commonwealth War Graves Commission (www.cwgc.org)
German: *Volksbund Deutsche Kriegsgräberfürsorge* (www.volksbund.de/graebersuche)
French: *Sépultures de guerre* website (www.sepulturesdeguerre.sga.defense.gouv.fr).
This website includes soldiers buried in military cemeteries or in the military plots of civilian cemeteries. It does not include fallen soldiers whose remains were returned to their families. For additional memorials, try the *Mémorial GenWeb* website (www.memorial-genweb.org).

War diaries of units
British: The National Archives, Kew, Richmond, Surrey TW9 4DU (www.nationalarchives.gov.uk)
French: *Mémoire des hommes* website (www.memoiredeshommes.sga.defense.gouv.fr/jmo/pages/index)

Other useful addresses
Neufmontiers *mairie*: *Place de la mairie*, 77124 Chauconin-Neufmontiers (www.chauconin-neufmontiers.fr)

INDEX

Entries are filed word-by-word. **Bold** locators refer to colour plate numbers. *Italic* locators refer to page numbers of other illustrations.

111, 113; 9th, 111; 13th,
125, 135; 14th, 122, 123–4,
125, 130, *131*; 15th, 124,
131
Cavalry regts: 4th Dragn
Gds, 9, 110; 5th Dragn
Gds, 115; 18th Hussars,
110
Infantry battalions: Grenadier
Gds, 2nd Btn, *99*, 103, 104,
105; Coldstream Gds, 2nd
Btn, 104, 105, 106;
Coldstream Gds, 3rd Btn,
102, 103, 106, 114; Irish
Gds, 1st Btn, 102, 103,
106; Black Watch, 1st Btn,
117; Cameron
Highlanders, 1st Btn, 117;
Cameronians (Scottish
Rifles), 1st Btn, *142*;
Connaught Rangers, 2nd
Btn, 112; East Lancashire,
1st Btn, 144; Essex, 2nd
Btn, 136; Highland Light
Infantry, 2nd Btn, 104–5,
106; King's Own (R.
Lancaster Regt), 1st Btn,
134; Lancashire Fusiliers,
2nd Btn, 136;
Lincolnshire, 1st Btn, 123,
123, 132–3; Queen's Own
(R. West Kent Regt), 1st
Btn, 140–1; Royal Irish,
2nd Btn, 113; Royal Scots,
2nd Btn, 113; Royal
Welch Fusiliers, 2nd Btn,
138; Worcestershire, 2nd
Btn, 104, 105, 114

Other corps or units: Royal
Artillery, 100, 102, 104,
105, 106, 107, 109, 112,
114–15, 124, 125–6; Royal
Engineers, 123, 141–3,
142; Royal Flying Corps,
121, 126; Field
Ambulances, 130, 133
Brodhag, S/Lt Eugène, 162, 172
Broussy-le-Grand, 173
Broyes, 175, 189
Bury, Cpl Henri, 47

Cardin, MdL Antoine, 165, *166*,
167
Caroly, Henri, 40–1, *41*
Cauchi, Lt Eric, 144
Cazalas, Capt Jean-Marie, 160
cemeteries, military: British,
133–4, 143–5, 208 (plots in
civilian cemys, 113–14, *114*,
115, 117, 132); French, 54–5,
65, 71, 84, 89, *89*, 92, *93*, 144,
172, 189, 191, 208 (*see also*
Grande tombe); German,
14; 54–5, 156–7, *174*, 191, 208
Châlons-en-Champagne
(Châlons-sur-Marne), 13,
207
Chambry, **9–10**; 55–6, *56*
Chamigny, 122, 135–7, *136*
Chamoust, 124, 125
Champain, Henri, 64
Champfleury farm (Tour 2),
66–7
Champfleury farm (Tour 3), 80,
81, 87
Charbonneau, Capt Jean, 194